SILVER & SAWDUST
Life In The San Juans

KEN REYHER

WESTERN REFLECTIONS
PUBLISHING COMPANY

First Edition

Printed in the United States of America

ISBN 1-890437-45-X

Library of Congress Catalog Number 00-105544

Cover and Design by SJS Design (Susan Smilanic)

Western Reflections Publishing Co.
P.O. Box 710
Ouray, Colorado 81427

Life in the Early San Juan Mining Towns
Preface

As early as the sixteenth century Spanish explorers began searching for gold and silver in the rugged San Juan Mountains. How much they found is open to question but they did leave behind mine shafts, abandoned tools, and legends. Mountain man and trapper Kit Carson made at least one trip into the San Juans and believed they contained gold and silver. Survivors of the ill-fated Fremont expedition who had attempted to cross the San Juans in the winter of 1848 came out insisting they had found gold near present day Creede, but no one returned to follow up. In 1860 small parties of gold seekers entered the San Juans, but the small amount of metal they found excited no one. Prospectors came again in 1869; this time, in the valley where the town of Silverton would emerge, they found small quantities of placer gold just enough to expand the search and to petition the federal government for a treaty with the local Ute Indians who occupied western Colorado. In 1873 the Brunot Agreement allowed prospectors access to more than three and a half million acres in the heart of the San Juans, and prospectors began pouring in. They found gold but it was silver that made the San Juans; silver in incredible quantities along with copper, lead, zinc, and manganese. Such wealth came at a high cost. Most mines were located above timberline and were prone to being flooded with acid-impregnated waters capable of eating away pipes, pumps, and tools in a matter of days. Winter snows piled as deep as sixty feet and deadly avalanches were common. Food, coal, and mining and building equipment were brought in with pack animals over some of the highest and most rugged terrain in North America. Towns and supply centers were built, along with reduction mills and smelters.

This is the story of those who accomplished these tasks. Many were veterans of the Civil War both north and south. They were joined by immigrants from several European countries including Wales, Finland, and Italy; veterans of Europe's tin and copper mines. Although differing in cultures, customs, and languages, these San Juan miners shared a vitality and a sense of almost reckless optimism. Together with mule skinners, shopkeepers, craftsmen, and others, they became united in a quest for wealth. This is the story of how they and their families lived, worked, played, and died during the glory years of San Juan silver.

Book Acknowledgments

The following people gave their time and expertise to help make this book possible. Gretchen Elsa Hamlett, Mary Roberts and Reigh Stoddard, all from the Delta County Library in Delta, were incredibly helpful in locating and obtaining reference materials. Dr. Doris Gregory, whose own books about southwestern Colorado have been both inspiration, and research sources, supplied many of the newspaper accounts. Dr. H. J. Scarinzi, a life-long family physician from rural eastern Colorado provided material, and advice pertaining to medical history during the last half of the nineteenth century. Marilyn Cox, curator of the Montrose Historical Museum in Montrose, provided access to important mining materials, and made available a number of previously unpublished photographs. Ann Hoffman, curator of the Ouray County Historical Museum in Ouray, arranged for similar services along with museum volunteer Sue Babcock who spent many hours searching for just the right pictures. Ron Sunderland of the *Delta County Independent* newspaper graciously gave his time electronically reproducing and enhancing photographs that had become fragile and dim with age. Nancy Lamm of Olathe produced the map. Publisher and author P. David Smith helped guide this project from inception to print. My sincere thanks. Ken Reyher

1

TABLE OF CONTENTS

CHAPTER ONE – *Tents to Towns*   *5*

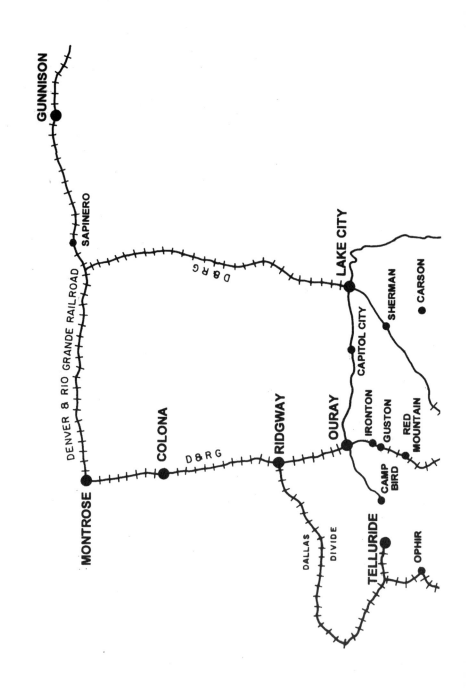

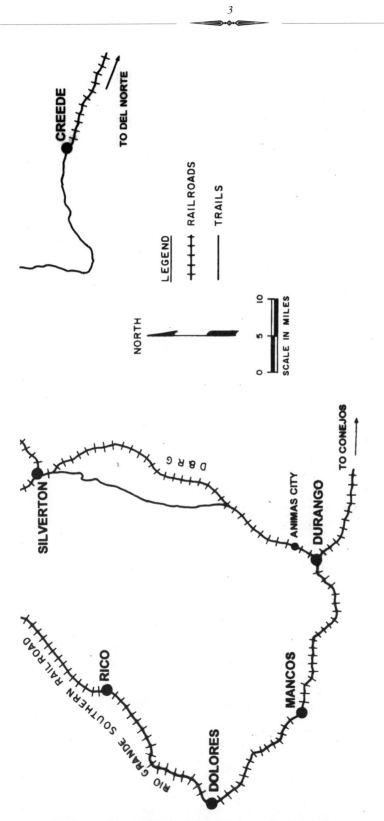

CHAPTER ONE –
Tents to Towns

The establishment of mining towns in the San Juan Mountains of southwest Colorado followed the patterns laid down years earlier across the American west. They were placed as close as possible to newly discovered mines and located to take advantage of available transportation routes. Both of these requirements meant they faced extreme challenges in the San Juans. Most of the ore bodies were found at or above timberline, in numerous cases as high as 13,000 feet above sea level. That put many workings a mile or more above the camps and towns that supported them. An added problem was that roads or trails from towns to mines were incredibly rough and steep. This proved to be a challenge of immense proportions when moving supplies, equipment, and ore. The same difficulty with terrain carried over to the location of town sites. San Juan valleys were deep and narrow and had few routes in or out. In addition the steep valley walls were avalanche prone. On occasion, entire towns disappeared beneath the thunder of thousands of tons of snow and ice.

These difficulties aside, the San Juaners went ahead and built. In many cases their handiwork lasted only a few years. Capitol City, located a few miles west of Lake City, was named with the optimistic hope it would one day replace Denver as the state capital. Like so many towns in the San Juans, Capitol City quickly died when nearby mines were depleted.

Other towns did survive through luck, circumstance, and their ability to adapt to changing times. Silverton, Ouray, Lake City, and Telluride are primary examples. Peripheral cities such as Durango, Montrose, and Gunnison that originally depended on the mining industry went on to establish their own unique niches in the economy of western Colorado.

Town sites began with a formal survey. Often only a limited amount of reasonably level ground was available. The first inhabitants lived in canvas tents painted with linseed oil to keep out the summer rains. They avoided wet ground by laying log floors and packing the cracks between with sand and gravel. In some cases log walls were raised four or five feet with a tent roof (sometimes over board frames) placed above. Interior walls consisted of canvas, unused blankets, or quilts. Such quarters served adequately during the warmer months, but San Juan winters required something more substantial. Log cabins were easiest to build. Trees on site were the first to be used, and after that logs were skidded in and sold for fifty cents each. Cabin roofs were made of smaller logs covered with left-over branches and other debris and then covered with a foot of dirt. The cracks between the logs were filled with a mixture of sand, water, and burro manure. Although small, cramped, and dark, such structures turned away the winter cold and were easy to keep warm. A new town's first winter was nearly always its hardest.

By spring of the second year, a town's growth began in earnest. At least one sawmill provided rough-cut lumber. Trees were felled and fed directly into the saws, loaded onto wagons and hauled to the building sites to be unloaded and weighted down with rocks to help delay warping.

Even so, such wood had to be used as quickly as possible because as it began to dry, it bent and twisted so badly as to become unusable. Shrinkage was an additional problem. One disgruntled home builder in Creede complained that the wood he had bought was so green his 15 x 20 foot cabin had shrunk to a 12 x 16. A recent arrival to Creede, not yet wise to San Juan humor, measured the structure and found that it did measure out to the smaller size.

An original, restored cabin at the Ouray County Museum. Author's Collection.

Most private dwellings were simple, two-room structures typically about 10 x 22 feet. Foundations were either non-existent or little more than flat rocks piled up to keep the house off the ground. In some cases a building was actually sunk a few inches into the ground. Wall frames were nailed up with studs placed on either thirty-six or forty-inch centers. Green boards a foot or more wide and one inch thick were nailed into place vertically around the outside. Smaller strips of lumber were nailed over the cracks between the larger boards. The process was known as board and batten construction. Roofs were open rafters which were shingled over. Doors and windows were often available from a local sash and door manufacturer, but homemade glass window frames and plank doors were common. During its first year, 1876, Ouray had two facilities devoted to making doors and window frames, and they were hard pressed to keep up with demand. Nails cost twenty-five cents a pound and were used sparingly. As the wood in the house walls continued to shrink, the inhabitants packed sawdust between the cracks to help keep out the wind and snow. Such structures were seldom painted because rough cut lumber absorbed expensive paint like a sponge. Taking advantage of the availability of sawed lumber, owners of log cabins frequently removed the cabin roof and added a second story. During the first few years of a town's existence, residential quarters were always in short supply. In 1875 a traditional two-room house in Silverton rented for forty dollars per month (the equivalent of nearly 1,000 dollars at 2000 present day prices), and there was always a waiting list of potential renters.

Many people added rooms to take in boarders. Such an arrangement could bring in up to eight dollars a week for an enterprising miner's wife who didn't object to feeding and caring for an additional household member. During the warmer months many young, single miners and construction workers camped out on the hillsides surrounding the towns. If he was willing to subsist on fried beef, lard biscuits, coffee, and dried fruit, a prudent camper could get by on two dollars a week. Prospectors and miners, further from town, spent the warmer months in crude brush or log shelters often built against a cliff or large vertical rock. In winter they were forced to move to town.

Business construction was similar to that of private homes especially regarding poor or missing foundations. Most main street buildings were built on lots twenty-five feet wide. Frequently they shared side walls with adjoining buildings to save construction costs and almost always boasted a false front. Business owners painted the fronts of their buildings with white lead-based paint to give contrast to the darker paints used for the business name and other advertising. Within two or three winters, coal smoke and nearby smelter fumes oxidized the white paint to a dingy gray, making the buildings appear to be much older than they were.

In many instances the deterioration did not matter because disastrous fires often leveled entire business districts. The practice of all-wood construction coupled with the sharing of common walls made for difficult conditions if a fire got started. Winters were the most dangerous because coal stoves and chimneys often belched hot sparks and live cinders. Of all the San Juan mountain towns, only Silverton and Ouray escaped disastrous business district fires. Durango suffered the worst conflagration when eight complete blocks of the downtown district burned to the ground July 2, 1889. High winds fed the Durango fire, and there was little the citizenry could do but stay ahead of the flames and empty what buildings they could of their contents.

Fires usually led to the second phase of a San Juan mining town's life. Replacement structures went up with an eye towards fire containment. Ceilings were covered with ornate, pressed iron panels, still visible today in many surviving structures. It was hoped that a metal barrier would provide for better fire containment. The theory did not work. External construction frequently turned to brick or stone. After a few years, most towns had a local brick yard, and many times former stone cutters from Europe found they could make a better living at their old occupations than they could at mining.

The mines also needed numerous on-site structures. There were many mines too far from the towns for daily commuting, so housing was erected for the married workers. Piles of mine rubble were leveled out on a mountainside; pilings were driven into the debris, and two-room houses similar to those in the towns were put up. Single workers lived in company boarding houses often located no more than a few yards from the mine itself. For many the construction business was as lucrative or even more so than mining. One young carpenter in Ouray stayed with the business, formed his own company, and amassed a fortune of nearly one hundred thousand dollars by his twenty-fifth birthday – a considerable sum for that day. Carpenters supplemented their incomes by making furniture when inclement weather kept them indoors. Prior to the coming of the railroads, factory-made home furnishings were prohibitively expensive to freight into the San Juan towns.

Early builders were also heavily into material recycling. When a building was no longer of any use at its original location, it was either moved or torn down and the materials were used again to build barns or other out-buildings. Ashes and debris from burned structures were raked clean of nails which were straightened and used again. Abandoned cabins were salvaged for whatever wood could be used for construction purposes, and anything left over was sawed up into firewood. Coal, although the fuel of choice in the San Juan towns, was expensive so wood, especially scrap wood, was burned in heating and cooking stoves whenever possible. Mothers sent their children on wood foraging expeditions and after the surrounding hillsides had been scoured clean, attention was focused on the alleys and dumps of the towns. Any stray piece of wood, and some that was not, ended up being carried home by young wood scroungers.

Towns that survived the initial years in the San Juans often underwent a final building phase. Flush with profits derived from business and mining interests, entrepreneurs built elaborate hotels, fraternal lodges, opera houses, hospitals, schools, and a variety of other civic buildings. These were almost always made of brick or stone and many are still in use today. One example is St. John's Episcopal Church in Ouray.

The building was constructed of thick double walls of native stone. Space left between the walls was filled with sawdust to provide insulation. The building is still used for regular worship services, and visitors can step inside and see the remarkable craftsmanship of more than a century ago.

Many of the individuals who participated in the construction of public buildings also turned their attention to home building on a more elaborate scale. The availability of brick led to the construction of many fine homes built in a style that came to be known as Victorian Bonanza. Partly due to constraints in lot size, most were not built on the grand scale of such homes in places like Denver, but what they lacked in size was usually made up in both external and internal opulence. Gingerbread trim laced the eaves,

French windows graced the walls, and turrets sprouted from the roofs. Even the outhouses were built to match the main structure with brick walls and a cupola on top. For the more modern minded, indoor bathrooms were available. As many as three might be found in some of the fancier homes along with imported hardwood floors, central heat, and electric lighting. It was the San Juan region of Colorado that pioneered the use of electricity in the mines, and electric power was also quickly adapted for residential use. Interior decoration was strictly Victorian. The Waldheim Mansion in Silverton, long since gone, had massive amounts of wood trim throughout the structure, and the furniture in each room was of a different and exotic hardwood. The same home had its own built-in bank vault.

Even those citizens who were less well-heeled often made improvements to their homes. Original log houses were upgraded in terms of doors, windows, and roofs, and the exterior logs were covered with siding. Many of those homes are still in use today. Owners began painting the portions of their houses that faced the street. Within ten years of their founding, most San Juan towns had progressed from board-and-batten construction to brick and stone. By 1885 most San Juaners were convinced they had a long and profitable future ahead of them, and that confidence became evident in the construction of their towns. Builders had also caught up with demand. The two-room shack that had rented for forty dollars a month in Silverton fifteen years earlier was a thing of the past. In 1890 a new seven-room frame rental home in Ridgway was advertised in the local paper for thirty-five dollars a month.

Buildings alone did not make a town. People living in proximity to each other needed a municipal government. A variety of problems had to be dealt with that were often unique to the San Juans. The mining camps and towns that sprang up across the western United States more than two decades earlier had been inhabited primarily by a transient male population. In contrast the San Juan boom attracted substantial numbers of families. As a result a region often went from mining camp to established town within a matter of months. Governing bodies were usually elected during the first few weeks. Typically among the first ordinances passed was one requiring building lot owners to remove tree stumps from the streets that bordered their properties. Procrastinators were fined.

Streets were a particular problem. Iron-bound wagon wheels ground the dry dirt into powder that erupted into clouds of choking dust with each puff of wind. Town officials hired an employee to keep the dust watered down with a barrel on a cart and a gravity fed sprinkler attached to the back. During rainy periods the same wagon wheels turned the streets into quagmires. One advantage during wet weather was that the prodigious quantities of horse, mule, burro, and ox manure that had been piling up on the streets was diluted, washed away or ground into the mud. The disadvantage was that when the street began to dry out, the same wagon wheels left deep ruts. The solution was to give miscreants from the city jail a wheel barrow and shovel and put them to work. A miner made an average of three dollars a day on the job. Jail sentences were worked off at one dollar a day and when the streets needed work, civic minded judges saw to it that the necessary labor was available.

Water, in one form or another, was a continuing municipal problem. Most towns were built along the banks of local rivers, but mining activities upstream quickly contaminated them to the point of being unusable for domestic consumption. Upriver residents also used rivers as dumping places for garbage, chamber pots, and other unsavory waste. In some cases outhouses were built directly over a running stream. These streams being outside municipal jurisdiction, there was very little a town could do to remedy these problems. As a result domestic water was drawn from springs (in some cases several miles away), and people either hauled their own or relied on local water carriers who found they could make a respectable living hauling barrels of water and making daily deliveries to homes and businesses within the town. Often these same springs were eventually ditched or piped (with wooden pipes) into town for domestic livestock use and to provide water in case of fires.

Garbage and trash were perennial problems in the San Juan towns. Many home owners kept livestock in the back yard, including a pig or two. Household leftovers were fed to these animals which, upon maturity, ended up feeding the household. Dogs ate table scraps and gnawed on discarded bones. Burros were also scavengers and had a special affinity for eating the greasy burlap sacks that had wrapped bacon and hams. They ate yard plants and, in some instances, clothing off the clothes line. A fenced yard became a necessity. In the early years garbage odors helped draw bears into the towns, but with large populations of dogs and residents with firearms, that problem usually ended up on someone's dinner table. Rendered bear fat was a great favorite for making biscuits, and miners would just as soon eat a bear roast as eat pork.

Garbage also drew rats and mice. Cats were rare in the San Juan towns. Many dogs having never seen their domestic cousins would kill them on sight. Skunks that made the mistake of coming into town met the same fate – and they left yet another smell to the already over-burdened air. A small dog that proved to be a good ratter was a sought-after commodity.

Unfortunately dogs, burros, and pigs could not consume everything and whatever was inedible was, from time to time, raked up and burned – adding even more variety to the odors of smoke, manure, and smelter fumes. It was said that a newcomer could tell a mining town's age by the amount of rusting tin cans and bottles scattered about.

Common sense and expediency set the ground rules for most laws and ordinances. Finances depended on license fees and sin taxes mostly. Silverton was typical. Each saloon and dance hall had to purchase an annual operating license for $500. Houses of prostitution were charged as much as $5.00 a month for each girl on the premises who had rendered services for all or part of that month. With dozens of such businesses in operation, town officials usually had enough revenue to pay the wages of several town employees and purchase whatever supplies the town needed. Each municipality retained the services of a local attorney, usually at a flat rate of $25.00 per month. It was the attorney who drew up ordinances and represented the town in the case of lawsuits. Laws included regulations against hogs and sheep at large, and a perpetual problem revolved around dogs. Miners who came to town on Saturday usually brought their animals with them, and while owners whiled away the evening in a saloon, dance hall, or other place of entertainment, the dogs waited outside, often in packs. They fought each other, sometimes threatened passersby and urinated and defecated wherever it pleased them. The town marshal spent a considerable portion of his time dealing with canine complaints. On occasion some of the towns attempted to pass dog-at-large ordinances, but the idea was a century ahead of its time. Only during summers of a rabies scare did the dog problem diminish. At such times a roaming animal might be shot on sight.

Another common ordinance dealt with explosives. Almost every town prohibited home or business storage of more than fifty pounds of blasting powder or dynamite giant powder as it was called then. The reason was fire. Even fifty pounds of explosives was capable of leveling several buildings, but mining and blasting were a part of everyday life, and a certain amount of risk was considered acceptable. Large quantities of explosives were stored either at mine sites or in special stone buildings outside the towns. Such a structure can still be seen today south of Ouray on the way to Box Canyon Falls.

To deal with the fire danger it was necessary to either purchase or make a hook and ladder truck. Since factory-made trucks cost $800 plus $200 shipping, most towns made their own. In its most simple form, such a vehicle consisted of a light, long bodied wagon that contained ladders and long poles with hooks on one end. Several dozen buckets were attached down each side. Volunteers pulled the vehicles to the fire and bucket brigades were formed to help contain the blaze. The hooks (attached to long wooden poles), in conjunction with the ladders, were used to pull down flimsily built wooden walls. In winter when water was not available, hooks and ladders were often the only option.

Another problem mining towns had to deal with was street traffic. Wagons, carts, horses, mules, burros, and oxen formed a volatile mix on the busy streets of a boom town. Accidents were common and sometimes deadly. In one instance a runaway team in Ouray ran into another team broadside. The tongue of the wagon the first team was pulling penetrated completely through both horses of the second team killing them both. To avoid such mishaps, ordinances were passed against acts that might frighten animals. The indiscriminate discharge of firearms was forbidden for that reason. Even children found themselves affected. It was against the law to fly kites, play ball, or roll hoops in and on streets when animal traffic was present.

As the San Juan mining towns grew, local governments played an ever expanding role. Ouray, founded in 1876, constructed a city water works one year later and by 1878 had built, in conjunction with Lake City and Silverton, a telephone system linking the three towns. From tents to bricks, water pipes, and telephones, the San Juan towns were quickly coming of age.

CHAPTER TWO –
Coming of Age

In less than two years, towns like Ouray, Silverton, Telluride, and Lake City became thriving metropolises of the San Juans. They were vibrant, pulsing entities with a way of life unique to the soaring mountains of southwestern Colorado. Few inhabitants were beyond the age of forty-five and optimism fueled the fires of exploration and discovery. Youth provided the muscle to tunnel and blast through to the rich veins of silver, copper, zinc, lead, and gold that had lain hidden since the great volcanic fires of ages past had burned out and grown cold.

If it can be said that each collection of homes and businesses had a heartbeat, the pulse could be detected in the local newspapers. No town or camp was considered complete without at least one printer. Usually it was the newspaper that installed the first wooden floor in camp (made necessary because of the heavy iron printing equipment). The editor, through his paper, served many functions. He presented both local and regional news. He was often one of the town's biggest boosters and a virtual one-man chamber of commerce. (On rare occasions there were lady editors, and they proved as capable and pugnacious as their male counterparts.) He could be, and often was, the most outspoken individual in town, barred from saying what he pleased only by his fear of being thrashed by some irate victim of his literary barbs. Suing a mining camp editor was usually an exercise in futility because most of them came to town broke and remained that way throughout their tenure. Editors did keep their verbal pomposity in check partly by the realization that their livelihood depended on advertising and revenue from public notices. Whenever temporary lapses of literary sanity did occur, most citizens ignored it. After all the better light the local paper cast on the area, the more people would move in, the better business would be, and the bigger the town would grow. Like rat terriers after their prey, editors of one town frequently launched verbal barrages at neighboring towns all in an effort to make their own community look better.

Best known of all the San Juan newspapermen was David Frakes Day. He began his adult life as a fifteen-year-old Union Army volunteer. Discharged four years later, he had suffered four wounds and had won the Congressional

Medal of Honor, all before the age of nineteen. He entered the newspaper trade by accident and ended up in Ouray where, over the span of a decade, he was sued for libel forty-two times. His adversaries never collected a cent. Day was said to have no use for con-games, self-serving politicians, or dishonest mining promotions. At one point he toured Europe and met the venerable Queen Victoria of Great Britain who took an instant liking to the bombastic editor and subsequently subscribed to his paper, *the Solid Muldoon.*

Day frequently promoted Ouray at the expense of surrounding towns. On June 8, 1883, the Muldoon had this to say about Silverton:

> No country is more picturesque and quaint than Silverton. There is something so novel in the long undulating rows of charcoal pits dotted here and there by innumerable tin horns, foraging for time-checks.
>
> The buildings are mostly of the Gothic order, and the roads carefully adorned with empty peach cans, Budweiser bottles and other imported statuary. The population is about 400,000, 399,500 of whom have not yet arrived, and the remaining 500 are Chinamen and dance house rustlers. The principal industry is gall, large quantities of which are annually shipped to Durango...

Editors from towns targeted by Day's literary pugilism were quick to fire back in terms of what they thought of the Ouray editor and his own place of residence. On a more positive note, the *Mining Register* at Lake City wrote these words to see in the new year with its January 1, 1881, issue:

> Our grand mountain canyons echo today with the music of the school and church bell, while the clatter of the busy printing press is heard in every camp and the smoke from the smelters and mills veil the snow-clad summits of our towering mountains...

A few weeks later, March 12, 1881, the *Durango Record Weekly* placed in print a problem common all across the San Juans.

> We have mineral enough and plenty of coal, and oxide of iron. The only lack of our resources is those potent civilizers of their pioneer brothers – the girls.

At that time Durango boasted a population of 2,500 people. The article sparked two female replies: one from Massachusetts and a second from St.

Louis – the latter stated her willingness to come to Durango but on the condition she could be guaranteed a wealthy bachelor between the ages of twenty-eight and thirty-eight.

For the most part the San Juan papers stuck to the day-to-day happenings in and around the vicinity. There was always interest in new mines opening, how much ore was being shipped, and when stores had received new consignments of food, clothing, or supplies. Notices concerning meetings, public gatherings, and local gossip appeared in each issue. It wasn't uncommon for an editor to note the passing of a particularly well known horse, burro, or town dog.

Married women put their own unique stamp on each community. They insisted on picket or board fences around their homes to keep out wandering livestock, especially the voracious burros that freely wandered the streets. They planted shrubbery and whatever garden plants would grow in the high, thin air and short summers of the San Juans. If nothing else they tended pots of geraniums, bringing them in during bad weather, wintering them over, and sharing cuttings with neighbors who also wanted to bring a spot of brightness into their homes. They had problems with mud, manure, snow, and ice. Bedbugs were common, and housewives frequently fought open wars with pack rats that would gain entrance to a home and carry off small household items. Retaliation came when the children would be sent out to find the offending rat's nest and retrieve the pilfered objects. The nest, usually consisting of a substantial collection of small sticks, made excellent kindling for the kitchen stove.

Mining towns did have social differences that a pot of geranium cuttings could not bridge. Although each municipality contained substantial numbers of married men with families, the majority of citizens were single males. When not working, many could be found in the saloons, dance halls, and houses that traded in the pleasures of the flesh. As a result 'nice' was restricted to one well defined side of town and 'vice' contained in the other two separate societies, each of which went its own way. Although discreet married males could cross from one side to the other with a reasonable amount of impunity.

Additionally, on the nice side of town, segregation sometimes resulted from cultural differences. American-born inhabitants tended to live close to each other while European immigrants frequently formed their own neighborhoods. Families from Wales and Italy, in particular, maintained a cultural separation. The fact that the former were Protestants and the latter Catholics made the division line more distinct. Time, shared experiences, and the interaction of children tended to blur even religious differences as the towns matured.

For the most part a basic level of democracy was in evidence because nearly everyone was a recent arrival. Because many people, both single and family units, tended to be transient, a custom evolved that was unique to the San Juans. When a family relocated any distance, they sold their house with most of the furniture, and sometimes their domestic livestock, other than horses and burros, as well. It was hoped that when they arrived in a new camp or town, replacement living quarters could be found furnished similarly to the ones they had left behind. The reason for this tradition was that wagon roads did not exist across most of the San Juans, and everything had to be packed by mule or burro – a process both difficult and expensive.

Many mining town homes had pits dug underneath the house, accessible through trap doors, and deep enough to ward off the freezing temperatures of winter an important reason, other than convenience, for these pits being inside the house. Packed with sawdust, they were used to store apples, potatoes, onions, pumpkins, and kegs of dill pickles and sauerkraut. During winter nights when fires were allowed to die down, interior temperatures in many homes would easily dip below freezing. In the spring of the year the pits were filled with ice and used to store milk, butter, and other heat-sensitive food items. Families with children considered a cow almost a necessity. During the summer and fall an older boy would come by each morning after milking, pick up the family cow and along with perhaps a dozen other milk cows, would head on up into the high meadows to let them graze for the day. He would return each cow by milking time that evening. It was a six-day-a-week job, and the herder was paid one dollar a month per animal. During winter and spring, livestock were kept at home and fed hay. New families, often unable to purchase adult animals, bought young ones or procured orphaned animals to raise. In the latter case, if milk was not available, alfalfa hay was soaked in a bucket of warm water for several hours making what was called hay tea. The liquid was poured off, warmed, and bottle-fed to orphaned colts, calves, and lambs.

Chickens were desirable as well. Because of wandering dogs they had to be penned, and each spring homemakers would place eggs beneath setting hens. This provided fresh frying chickens later in the summer and replacements for the laying flock. Many women liked to kill a bird and take it down to the creek or river to clean it. Feathers, offal, and other unusable parts were allowed to float on downstream. As towns grew and social censure increased, such practices died out.

The site selected for Lake City was bare ground in 1874, but less than eighteen months later there were 300 homes, fifty-seven businesses (including nine saloons), two millinery and dress shops, one jewelry store, a church, one fraternal lodge, a school, ten lawyers, and five doctors. More construction was underway.

Mining towns existed not only to provide labor and supplies for nearby mines but many of the physical and business amenities that were available in more settled regions. Lawyers nearly always outnumbered doctors two to one. Lawsuits were common because mining claims frequently overlapped

First grand jury of Ouray County - 1876. Courtesy Ouray County Historical Society.

and owners would fight it out in court as to where boundary lines should be. It was common for a mine to have several owners, and disagreements were frequent, especially when a property was sold. These problems were also dealt with in court. In addition business establishments frequently changed hands several times a year, or bills were protested or left unpaid. All of this provided a fertile ground for attorneys.

The San Juan region was capital-poor during the early years. Banks were the only certain source of cash. All loans were short term, usually a year or less. Solid customers who had considerable assets could borrow money at eight percent. Most businesses were quoted rates of twelve percent and small personal loans cost as much as twenty-four percent per year. Banks were not generally trusted, so many people kept their cash hidden at home. A Lake City blacksmith built a secret compartment inside his big leather – covered bellows to store his excess money.

For most, however, there was never enough currency to meet the day-to-day obligations in commercial and personal transactions. As a result the mining towns and camps operated on credit. San Juan County attempted to issue scrip, but businessmen refused to accept it at face value and the experiment was dropped. Instead people had to trust each other. Packers and suppliers extended credit to shopkeepers, and shopkeepers extended credit to shoppers. The financial wheels of the San Juans were greased by a person's word and a simple handshake. If that did not work, the lawyers were summoned. Perhaps it was because of the necessity of the system that it was honored as well as it was. In one instance a woman who ran a boarding house in one of the camps between Lake City and Silverton had a boarder skip out without paying his bill. It was known that he had headed for Silverton so a half dozen of the woman's more upright boarders took the day off and went to Silverton. They found the man drinking in a saloon, waiting for the train to Durango. He made his connection but only after anteing up the unpaid boarding house bill and a penalty on the side, which the temporary bill collectors used to slake their own thirsts. Some people did skip town and left unpaid bills, but most business owners learned to factor this in by raising prices for everyone else. Lack of cash aside, the business of the San Juan merchants was business and, in that respect, they became masters of their craft.

With a high percentage of single miners, restaurants and cafes did a booming business. Five dollar meal tickets, purchased in advance, cut the cost of meals by as much as a third. Volume and an established clientele became the name of the restaurant game. To attract more diners, mining town eating houses vied for the services of the best cooks who could make half again what a miner could expect to earn. Many restaurants were open around the clock to accommodate the miners schedules. During the 1880s, a French cafe in Silverton operated on a twenty-four hour schedule and served a variety of imported fish, oysters on the half-shell, many kinds of wild game, and the very best liquors and cigars. Good money could be made in operating an eating establishment. In 1880 John Elitch crossed the San Juans on foot with a sheet iron stove strapped to his back. He began with a tent restaurant in Durango and for eight years saved his money. He relocated to Denver and established the world famous Elitch's Gardens. Every town had a bakery. Two years after its founding, Ouray had two; both produced a full line of baked goods and the Orendorf Bakery made daily deliveries to local eating establishments and private homes.

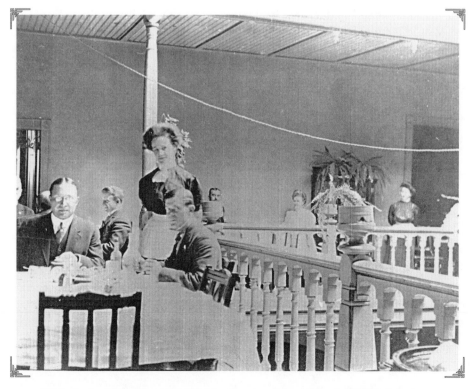

Diners in the Ouray Beaumont Hotel. Courtesy Ouray County Historical Society.

Telluride was typical in terms of operating hours. Stores opened at 7:00 a.m. and closed between 10:00 and 11:00 p.m. Most were open six days a week, but those that accommodated the mining crowd were open on Sundays as well. Some store owners offered rental storage space to miners and travelers for such things as saddles, guns, or other personal possessions they did not wish to take with them on a prospecting trip or up to the mines. Storekeepers frequently grubstaked prospectors with food and supplies for thirty days in return for half of whatever might be found. Nearly every businessman in a San Juan town, at one time or another, from bankers to bakers, invested money in prospecting or took time to scratch around in the surrounding hills in hopes of finding a strike.

Usually within the first two years of a town's existence, nearly everything could be purchased that would have been available in Denver but at a twenty-five percent mark-up from Denver prices, primarily because of high freight rates. Once railroads entered the area those costs came down. To meet demand, many shops and businesses entered niche markets. Barber shops sold tobacco products and other personal items not found in a Denver barber shop. Barber shops also doubled as bath houses for single miners. A man would come in Saturday afternoon and get a haircut, shave, shine, massage, shampoo, singe, and a bath.

Early road building crew. Courtesy Montrose County Historical Museum.

Harness shops frequently sold shoes and boots. One Silverton shoemaker gained national recognition by designing and patenting a sturdy mining boot called the Mann & Rankin. Most towns also boasted a resident tailor. It was not practical to purchase and ship large quantities of ready-made suits, so trousers and coats were made from material on hand and cost from thirty to forty-five dollars for the set; somewhat expensive but that helped cut down on saloon fights. Potential pugilists could seldom afford to ruin an expensive suit, and they did like to dress up on Saturday nights. Again to accommodate the large number of single miners, laundries were needed, and most towns had at least two, usually operated by Chinese proprietors. Clothing was washed in large tubs of boiling water and then dried and ironed. To remove the wrinkles, the Chinese ironer would take a mouthful of water and spew it across the item beneath his iron. The custom was not relished by most clients, but they had to put up with it or iron their own clothes.

Grocery stores were in abundance in the San Juan mining towns and even general merchandise stores stocked durable groceries. Fresh fruits and vegetables came from farms and orchards immediately outside the mountain areas. The Durango region supplied Silverton and its satellite towns. The Uncompahgre Valley took care of Ouray, Telluride, and camps in that locale. The valleys between Gunnison and Lake City served the eastern San Juans. Beef was provided by the same respective areas. Cattle were driven in from a valley ranch and held in pens behind a butcher shop to be processed out on a daily basis. There were only two popular cuts: boiling beef or steaks.

The distance from major supply points and severe winter weather often made for difficulties in keeping food on the table. During particularly severe winters it became almost impossible to get supplies into some of the towns. During the severe storms of 1880-81 restaurant meals in Rico reached a high price of $5.00 – up from fifty cents. Flour climbed to $50.00 per hundred pounds and eggs were $3.00 a dozen. Cattle were driven to within six miles of town where they were killed, quartered, and hauled the rest of the way on sleds. During the same period flour in Ouray, although more expensive than normal, was available for $11.00 per hundred pounds and eggs peaked at $1.25 a dozen.

Women had their own roles in the San Juan towns. Records from a millinery shop in Ouray during the year 1879 show that the town had forty-three married matrons and nineteen single women of integrity. Ladies of easy virtue were not counted, but their number probably equaled or surpassed that of their proper Victorian counterparts. Some women ran boarding houses, a respectable and profitable occupation. It was hard work and usually involved the employment of one or more female helpers to assist with cleaning, cooking, and serving. They did not do laundry. Most boarding houses averaged about twenty-five men who each paid $8.00 a week.

Many of the restaurants and cafes were owned and operated by women, and their profits almost always out-paced those of the average working male. Supplementing the restaurant trade were miners wives who sold fresh baked bread and pies to their husbands' co-workers who enjoyed taking such delicacies to work with them above and beyond their normal lunches.

The real money in mining towns was made in the saloon trade. In 1880 a surviving shipping invoice from Lake City shows whiskey selling wholesale at seventy-five cents a gallon. The same invoice listed a gallon of kerosene at double that amount. The whiskey sold retail for more than a 400 percent markup; the kerosene only a fraction of that amount. The town of Silverton literally began with saloons, six of them – and during the years that followed, the Silverton saloons on Blair Street remained open around the clock. Sunday was the biggest day because many of the mines closed. The town had its own brewing company with a spigot outside the brewery and a cup chained alongside, so that thirsty passersby could stop for a free quaff of beer. In 1890 Ouray counted thirty saloons and a brewing company which charged twenty-five cents for a half gallon of beer. Customers brought their own containers. Saloon patrons dropped a quarter on the bar, received a glass of beer and a twelve and a half cent token good for a refill. Most saloons offered free lunch counters which provided heavily salted snacks which encouraged patrons to buy even more beer.

So it was that the San Juan mining towns came into existence in a very short time. The speed at which they grew astonished even those who were there. The November 29, 1879, issue of the *Ouray Times* had this to say about the founding of Rico:

This place impresses one as having gotten there before it was sent for... wine and women, cards and caterers, houses and horses, men and burros, monkeys and mines, storms and stores, sawmills and gospel mills, carpenters and sign painters, assay offices and bunco steerers, Sunday schools and kino chambers.

A bit more tongue-in-cheek and with a touch of Victorian humor the August 5, 1904, *Ouray Plaindealer* had this to say about the speed at which things happened in the San Juans:

Once upon a time there was a young man and a young woman who read newspapers a great deal, including the advertisements. They ate Grape-nuts, Force, Quaker Oats and Uneeda Biscuits. He smoked Cremo cigars and drank Duffy's Malt Whiskey, while she quaffed Lydia Pinkham's Vegetable Compound and Syrup of Figs. The result was that they got married and were blessed with twins in less than six months, and lived happily ever after.

It is likely that at least a few readers bought the story after all, they had witnessed events almost as miraculous.

CHAPTER THREE –
Packers, Freighters and Iron Horses

The prospectors who came into the San Juans took immediate note of the soaring and almost forbidding terrain they encountered. At first they confined themselves to the narrow and winding valleys looking for placer gold. They found small quantities, but never enough to show solid financial promise. Then they raised their eyes upward towards the towering, cloud draped peaks. It was there that they found silver-incredible quantities of silver. But finding the white metal proved the easy part. Getting it out would tax the very limits of human ingenuity. Most of the ore bodies were at or above timberline, more than two miles above sea level. Heavy mining machinery had to be moved up to the mines and the ore had to be hauled back down. Working personnel usually lived at the site so building materials, food, and coal also had to be transported up the mountain. Supply centers were established in the valleys, and for the first few years, until railroads were built, everything needed had to be freighted in by wagon and then packed in on the backs of burros or mules for the final miles up to the diggings. Costs were high but not out of reason considering the logistics. But a mine could not hope to be successful unless its output in silver exceeded the cost of transporting supplies, materials, and ore. Packers and freighters didn't mind a challenge, and they approached the task with an inventive ingenuity that ultimately overcame most of the odds.

The diminutive burro stood at the apex of San Juan transport and continued to hold that position for more than a generation. California miners had first discovered the versatility of these creatures in 1849, and their use spread across the west in subsequent years. Descendants of Spanish donkeys, American southwestern burros were scruffy creatures who, through generations of indiscriminate breeding, were not exactly pretty to look at. They were short, stocky, paunch-bellied, shaggy, and lacked grace and any semblance of equine beauty. Prospectors called them Rocky Mountain canaries in deference to their distinctive bray which could be heard more than a mile away. But whatever cosmetic shortcomings these creatures had were more than made up in their ability to adapt as beasts of burden.

Burros were gentle creatures who were seldom a danger to anyone although they did have ways of protesting. Just prior to the moment when a packer would secure the pack saddle cinches around its belly, a burro would take air in and hold as much as it could. The savvy packer would kick

Pack train between Ridgway and Ouray. Courtesy Ouray County Historical Society.

the offending animal squarely in the stomach and as the beast exhaled, he quickly drew the cinches tight. Since they were not very high off the ground, burros were easy to pack. A standard load was 150 pounds split evenly on each side. If it was not distributed properly, burros could prove incredibly agile and either dump the load or work it off their backs and let it slide around to their bellies then stand patiently while the packer filled the air with curses and grudgingly reset the load. Burros could turn mean on occasion but usually gave ample warning by flattening their ears back on their heads. Odd loads had to be dealt with from time to time, and it was then that a packer could prove how skilled he really was. In 1875 one ingenious individual was seen leaving Del Norte, in the San Luis Valley, headed over the mountains towards Silverton with a full sized billiard table secured to twelve burros.

On the trail burros were allowed to run loose like sheep. They followed a lead animal, usually a wise old jenny who wore a bell. If terrain allowed, the train would travel in a 'V' formation which tended to crowd oncoming traffic off the road. When terrain dictated, the burros would string out single file in their own self-determined order. Many packers used dogs to help direct the train. A good burro-herding dog, when available, might sell for several hundred dollars. At end of day, the animals were unpacked and turned loose to graze. They could survive on a wide variety of vegetation, and by dark would return to camp where they would settle in for the night. Burros often competed as to which ones could gain positions closest to their human charges and the fire. Some packers even allowed favorite animals to

A burro train with a herd dog at upper right. Courtesy Ouray County Historical Society.

share their tents during stormy weather. The animals would head back out to graze at first light and would return on command in time to be reloaded for that day's work.

These diminutive animals were excellent foragers and did not require grain like their larger cousins, horses and mules. They required minimum

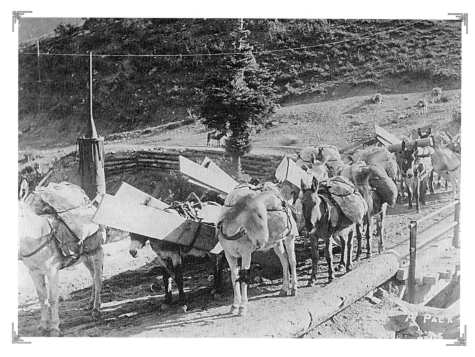

Supplies on the way to a mine. Courtesy Montrose County Historical Museum.

medical attention and did not have to be shod. Many times only burros could make it up the narrow, twisting trails that led to the higher mines. The *Solid Muldoon* reported to its readers during the summer of 1883 that as many as 400 burros a day could be seen heading out to the various workings located between Ouray and Red Mountain carrying supplies and lumber. However, as sturdy and dependable as the little beasts were, they had their limits and then pack mules became necessary.

Mules were crosses between female horses and male burros. They had the size and strength of their mothers and the brains and common sense of their fathers – as well as a few additional traits blended in for good measure. Mules could prove intractable, stubborn, and sometimes had tempers to match. They were also able to kick in directions a horse could not. They were expensive, needed grain and hay, and had to be shod – a ritual many did not submit to as willingly as their less head-strong cousin the horse. However, on the positive side, mules proved to be dependable, surefooted, less prone to panic than a horse, and could carry exceptional loads.

Normally the weight they packed going up the mountain averaged 250 pounds. Coming downhill a good mule was loaded with up to 350 pounds. On occasion, and for short distances, some animals could manage with up to 700 pounds tied to their backs. Even wagons were sometimes disassembled, loaded onto mules, and hauled into places they could never have gone on wheels.

"Mule skinners" were a special breed of men and proud of what they did, but their careers were often short. A well-placed kick could cripple a man for life and repeated lifting of heavy loads up onto the pack saddles left many a "skinner" suffering from multiple hernias. During an early Labor Day contest in Silverton, two packers loaded fifteen mules with sixty one-hundred-pound sacks of ore concentrate weighing a total of 6,000 pounds. Their winning time was four minutes and twenty-seven seconds. These and other dangers aside, such men took great pride in being able to haul almost impossible loads and they looked out for each other both on the trail and off. It was common knowledge never to mess with a mule skinner in a saloon altercation if other members of his occupational fraternity happened to be present.

Uncompahgre Valley farmers bailing hay for the mines.
Courtesy Montrose County Historical Museum.

Unlike burros, mules were tied head to tail, and the packer rode the lead animal. The final mule in the train wore a bell so that the packer would always know where that mule was on the blind and twisting trails. Longer trains utilized two men, the second man riding the last animal. Difficulties could arise if an ascending train met a descending train on a trail too narrow to pass each other. Packers kept their ears open for the sounds of other traffic and gave way to another string depending on available passing areas. Mules carrying heavy mining timbers, butt ends dragging along the ground, could not back up, so they always had the right of way. Normally a mule string would carry a variety of goods. A visitor descending from Ironton into Ouray recorded passing mules loaded with mining supplies, lengths of iron pipe, lumber, frozen sides of beef, and an empty coffin.

Ore wagons. Courtesy Montrose County Historical Museum.

Mules, with their longer legs and greater strength, could pack through deep winter snows, whereas their shorter legged cousins, the burros, could not. But cold weather packing was not without its problems. Extreme temperatures could result in frostbite both for packers and their animals. Loaded mules packed the trail down into almost solid ice and they would

A Dave Wood freight wagon. Courtesy Montrose County Historical Museum.

sometimes slip off into the nearby deep snow and become hopelessly bogged down. The packers would have to remove the load, help the animal back up onto the trail, and reset the packs. On occasion a mule would lose its footing and plunge head over hooves down a mountainside. Deep snow usually prevented injury, but the animal was unable to climb back up through the snow to regain the trail. It was either led on down the mountain, or if that was not possible, unpacked and left to get out on its own or perish. On particularly dangerous portions of a trail it was not uncommon after the snow had melted to see the rotting carcasses of pack animals strewn among the rocks below. Avalanches were a frequent danger and pack strings and their human charges were sometimes lost beneath a wall of white death. Packers were not cruel people, but they had a job to do and sometimes lives depended on whether they got through or not. On one occasion a mule train fought deep snow and high winds to bring food and other needed items to a mining camp south of Ouray. Upon arriving they found that there was no place to stable their exhausted animals. With night coming on the desperate packers finally located a two story bordello that had closed for the winter. In a short time they moved furniture and furnishings aside to make both floors available for their mules to crowd in and spend the night in relative comfort. Grateful that they had been able to save several thousand dollars worth of animals, the packers willingly paid for the damages the following spring when the madam and her girls returned.

Burros and mules were not the only traffic on the San Juan trails. Cattlemen from Durango, the Gunnison area, and the Uncompahgre Valley north of Ouray often contracted with the bigger mines to drive beef, on the hoof, up to the workings where they were placed in holding pens to be slaughtered out as needed. Cowboys discovered new challenges trying to drive valley-raised steers up a mountain trail. In the event the cattle would not accommodate their drovers, they would be held at a lower elevation, butchered, quartered, and loaded onto mules. One way or another hungry miners got their beef.

Stagecoach leaving Montrose for Ouray. Courtesy Montrose County Historical Museum.

People needed to travel too, and while most miners got from place to place on foot, there was a demand for horses. Mountain horses were almost always small and short-legged, traits that were desirable for traveling the narrow trails shared by burros and mules. Most San Juan towns had at least one stable where a saddle horse could be rented for round trips as well as one–way rides. In the case of the latter, a rider would arrive at his or her destination, tie the reins to the saddle horn, and turn the animal loose to find its way back to town and the home stable. The saddles of such animals were painted with the stable name so no one took any notice of these riderless horses returning to town on their own.

Freight wagons on the way to Telluride. Courtesy Montrose County Historical Museum.

Winter was the most challenging season for travel, and there were times and places where even the best pack animals could go no further. Mail carriers were the kings of the cold season. Required by government regulations to make a predetermined number of deliveries each week, these individuals sometimes achieved almost superhuman feats of endurance and perseverance. When the snow became too deep to wade through, the carriers strapped long, homemade wooden skis to their feet. They made their rounds with one stout pole to drag along through the snow to help turn and to control speed. To help supplement their income, mailmen would often carry specialty orders for customers, especially during times of shortages. It was not uncommon for a woman to pay a dollar for a mailman to bring her a roll of thread, itself costing just a few cents. Standard fees for a plug of tobacco averaged five dollars and a quart of whiskey might fetch upwards of fifty cents for every mile it was carried. Some mailmen used dog sleds to carry their winter mail and were able to carry a limited amount of freight. There were no regulations forbidding such ventures as long as the mail itself got through and on schedule. It was this regulation that often caused more problems than even deep snow because it forced mail carriers to travel during times when the avalanche danger was high. In March of 1886, mail carrier George Winders touched off an avalanche as he was going from Silverton to Telluride. He survived only to find that the slide had uncovered the remains of a previous carrier lost two years earlier. The intact mail sack was still strapped to the back of the unfortunate avalanche victim and was finally delivered more than two years late but still in excellent condition.

Miners also traveled during the snowy months. The *Solid Muldoon* reported, during an especially snowy winter, that one Dave Kelley came into Ouray, loaded a fifty pound sack of flour onto his back and then skied back to his cabin, eight miles away, four thousand feet higher in elevation all in three hours and through deep, soft snow.

During the early Silverton years, a German-born resident used three large, black dogs to pull a sled on which he transported six five-gallon cans of water around town to sell for five cents per can. His sled and dogs were also used to haul coffins to the cemetery when the snow was too deep to get there any other way. At the end of the working day each dog was given a stiff shot of whiskey and allowed to sleep in its owner's home.

Horse drawn sleighs were also relied on for transport around the towns in winter and, once roads were built, for travel beyond. This could prove a heart-stopping experience, especially on some of the winding, twisting, San Juan roads where the edges often dropped off hundreds of feet down vertical cliffs.

The lack of roads plagued the San Juans until a man named Otto Mears took it upon himself to begin connecting the region with what ultimately became a network of toll roads connecting most of the mining towns and camps. Mears had come to America as a Russian orphan not yet in his teens. He first landed at New York, and then went on to Panama where he made the treacherous jungle crossing to the Pacific side and booked passage on another ship to California where he worked as a freight handler, dairyman, and tinsmith. Always careful with his money, the teenager slept under porches and buildings to avoid having to pay rooming expenses. As a young man he joined the U. S. Army and was sent to New Mexico to fight the Navajo under the famed frontiersman, Kit Carson. From there he moved north into the San Luis Valley of Colorado, and, still in his early twenties, involved himself in several successful business ventures, one of which involved milling flour. When he found it impossible to get his product across the mountains in wagons, he solved the problem by building first one road and then another and charging others to use them as well. Throughout the 1870s, Mears and his road construction crews traversed the San Juans from one end to another, hacking and blasting their way through more than 200 miles of mountain terrain. Generally they tried not to exceed grades of twelve percent, and when possible, roads were eighteen feet wide. Of all his works, Mears took the most pride in opening a wagon road between Silverton and Ouray. Often clinging precipitously to the faces of sheer rock cliffs, this route was of vital importance to the mining towns and camps in the Red Mountain region. In places it was so narrow that nervous people on horseback would get off and lead their animals. Stagecoach passengers enthusiastically declared it to be the most terrifying road in the world. Travelers traverse the same route today over the famed Million Dollar Highway (greatly improved from Mears's day) still with a certain level of trepidation.

Building mountain roads was an expensive undertaking, and Mears set his tolls in accordance with what the market would bear, but fares were usually standard from one road to the next. A wagon could be charged up to five dollars depending on how many animals pulled it. Someone on a saddle horse passed for a quarter. Pack animals cost ten cents each as did cattle, sheep and goats although those fees could be higher. Travelers not used to paying tolls grumbled at the cost but even more at actual road conditions. Mears was often so busy building roads that he did not have time to maintain what was already built. Traffic and weather took a heavy toll, and at times some roads became next to impassable. On one occasion Mears himself came upon a wagon bogged down in deep mud near Lake City. He dutifully lent a hand and helped the two sweating and cursing teamsters get their vehicle on firmer ground, all the while listening quietly as they vented their fury towards both the road and its builder. As Mears rode away he told the pair that the man to whom they were referring would be riding that same road that very day, and they would surely have the chance to meet and converse with him. The two wagon men, unaware who it was they were talking to, thanked Mears profusely and the trio parted company.

Such complaints must have been frequent because at one point the *Ouray Times* reported to its readers that if some travelers' prayers were answered concerning the difficulty in traveling Mears's roads, the builder would receive a very hot reception when he entered the next world. But Mears had his supporters as well. On May 20, 1881, the Ouray paper *Solid Muldoon* had this to say: "Otto Mears is the one man in the San Juans who is always returning good for evil. He has done more than any other ten men in the country, and at the same time has been the recipient of more curses than even the Muldoon."

Whatever their condition, roads were vital to the San Juans, and wagons could move freight more economically and in far greater quantities than possible with pack animals. Freighters learned quickly that they needed to use heavier vehicles built to withstand the constant pounding of rough, rutted tracks and big rocks. The huge iron-bound, wooden wheels took the brunt of the abuse and were in constant need of repair. A mountain freight wagon weighed from four to five thousand pounds and could haul double its own weight. It was normally pulled by three teams, six huge Percheron/Belgian-cross horses. Oxen were preferred for extremely heavy loads with up to six teams, a total of twelve animals per wagon. Freighters had their own special problems. Wagons had very poor brakes, and to prevent them from overrunning the teams when going down hill, teamsters would attach a long rope to the rear of each vehicle and then run it several times around a nearby tree. As the wagon worked its way down the hill the rope would be played out. For years afterwards, dead trees lined the early roads, killed from ropes that had burned through the bark to the wood underneath. In some instances loads were transferred to sleds left at hilltops just for that purpose, then slid down to the bottom of the grade where the cargo would once again be loaded into the wagons. Coming up steep hills presented problems as well. When necessary, teams would be doubled or even tripled in order to provide enough motive power to gain the top. Sometimes a wagon tongue, unable to take the heavy strain, would break and the wagon, out of control, would roll back down the hill with disastrous results. Freight wagons, in order to have enough man-power, and horse-power usually ran in trains of eight to ten rigs.

Once freight reached its primary destination, it was unloaded and sent either by pack animals or ore wagons on up to the mines. Ore wagons were smaller than general freight vehicles and carried lighter loads but were just as sturdily built and pulled by two to three teams of either horses or mules. Ore haulers were often little more than teenagers or men in their early twenties, but they were experts and their own particular problems traversing steep, winding mountain roads. During good weather and easy runs they did not mind carrying a passenger or two, and women who lived at or near the mines often hitched rides to the town below to shop and get groceries. It was common courtesy that she supply the driver with a fresh pie or some other baked item in exchange for the ride.

Like the packers, ore haulers put bells on their teams to warn approaching traffic on blind curves. If their route was not too steep, a second man rode the wagon operating a long brake lever connected to oversized brakes attached to the rear wheels. When declines were too steep for brakes, drivers would chain their rear wheels so that they could not turn at all. This turned the rear half of their vehicle into a skid. In other instances they would drag a freshly cut tree, branches and all, if one was available. Many of the narrow roads to the mines tended to slope down towards the outside edge. When the surface became slick and muddy (and to prevent a wagon from sliding off the edge into an abyss below) chains were wound through the spokes and around the outer rim of each wheel, similar to tire chains today. In winter the ore wagon teams were shod with shoes that had short spikes on the bottom. These were secured by screw threads, much like a short bolt, and could be screwed out and replaced as they wore down without removing the animal's shoes.

Despite an improving transportation system, the San Juans were still at the mercy of winter weather. Conditions remained mild until 1883 when snows that, up to that winter, had seldom been more than two or three feet deep, suddenly increased to depths of ten feet or more. For the remainder of the decade rough winters were the norm, and many mines had to close during the worst months. Avalanches were frequent and deadly. During the spring of 1891 the Riverside Slide south of Ouray ran several times, ultimately covering 480 feet of the road. A tunnel was dug through the slide impacted area, and the snow and ice above it ultimately reached more than one hundred feet in depth. The tunnel was large enough to allow for stagecoach traffic and was still in use the following July. Problems continued throughout the San Juans as massive spring runoffs tore out bridges and washed away roads.   Moving freight under these conditions proved a Herculean task.

It was weather and its aftermath that made mining risky in the San Juans. Unpredictable natural events could raise freighting costs for a mine so high that its owners might quickly find themselves in bankruptcy. An 1880 diary account tells of one freighter who toiled for two weeks making less than one mile a day. In addition there never were enough freighters to handle the incredible growth that was occurring in the mountains of southwestern Colorado. For those that did provide services, operating costs were high. A new freight wagon sold for about the same price as a nice home might sell for back east. Six mules, purchased in Gunnison, at 2000 prices sold for the equivalent of fifteen thousand dollars at today's prices. Stock had to be fed expensive hay and grain and during severe winters most of a freighter's stock was idle but still eating. At such times freighters with livestock quartered in Ouray, Silverton and Telluride were paying, the equivalent of more than seventeen hundred dollars a ton for hay and fifty cents a pound for grain. Stock not used during the winter was moved closer into the valleys where prices were considerably lower. The biggest freighter operating out of Montrose maintained more than 500 head of oxen, mules, and horses year around.

Employees were easier to deal with. Most of the teamsters, drivers, and freight handlers were simply let go during the most extreme winter months with the understanding their jobs would be waiting for them the following spring. Other employees stayed on but worked for reduced wages. For some that would not have been a problem. During the 1880s the highest paid craftsmen in the San Juans were wheelwrights, those men who repaired wagon wheels. Freight line owner Dave Wood paid his chief wheelwright in Montrose twenty-two dollars a day, more than seven times the daily wage of a miner.

Until the railroads came, freighters generally made money and lots of it. In late 1881 it cost shippers three and one-half cents per pound to transport freight from the rail head in Gunnison to Montrose. It cost almost another penny a pound to move it from Montrose to Ouray. Most freighters contracted their services to either mining interests or businesses operating in the mining towns. This fact made it difficult for private parties to bring in personal belongings and home furnishings. If private shippers did want something brought in – and that was common – they paid substantially higher rates.

Once cargo reached a major mountain supply town, it was unloaded and repacked onto animals or piled into ore wagons and hauled on up to the mines. The big freight wagons would return to Montrose and then Gunnison with loads of high grade silver ore, which (because it took up less room and was easier to handle) traveled at half the price of regular freight. In some cases ore was processed into bullion at the mines and that was usually shipped out in the bottoms of freight wagons, hidden beneath a shipment of raw ore. With eight to ten wagons, at least that many heavily armed teamsters, and no publicity, attempts at robbery were almost non-existent. Very little San Juan silver ever moved by stage coach.

Merchants in Telluride, not wanting to order large quantities of winter merchandise too early in the fall, sometimes gambled and found themselves locked-in by early snows. Freight wagons could no longer move. Only the long-legged and dependable pack mules were able to fight their way through the early mountain snows. Even with reduced supplies brought in at a higher cost, Telluride survived.

Not only were packers and freighters dedicated to the task at hand, they would work around the clock if the situation demanded. Loads were expected to be picked up and shipped out within twenty-four hours after being unloaded at the railhead. That sometimes meant handling freight all night and then being on the road all next day. Demanding work schedules were routine but drinking on the job was not allowed, and abuse to either animals or equipment was not tolerated.

The efforts of San Juan freighters were impressive. In 1884 freighter Dave Wood (the biggest of several operators north of the San Juans) shipped 2,312,886 pounds of freight from Montrose to Ouray and another 1,516,171 pounds from Montrose to Telluride. An additional 765,688 pounds went to Fort Crawford, a military post a few miles south of Montrose. From Ouray and Telluride Wood's men hauled back to Montrose 3,215,090 pounds of ore. Attention to detail is most telling in an 1888 receipt Dave Wood's family saved from a citizen in Telluride who sent to Montrose an order for "enough peas to plant two rows 50 feet long, a few radish seed and a few lettuce seed." The order was filled and put on a wagon bound for Telluride.

One final group of men essential to San Juan freighting were the Hispanic teamsters out of Santa Fe and Taos. These individuals were experts with oxen and knew how to deal with exceptionally heavy loads. Specialized pieces of mining equipment, such as pumps, boilers, and steam engines that weighed several tons, were attached to the running gear of heavy wagons and moved along with ten teams of oxen up steep grades considered almost impossible by casual observers. In such situations, when exceptional pulling power was needed, as many as twenty teams would be used – forty animals in all. Loads, often hanging precariously close to the edge, would literally inch their way upwards to the mines. One miscalculation, one slip, and a fortune in irreplaceable equipment could easily plunge down the face of a mountain dragging both men and animals to their deaths. These New Mexico specialists were so reliable that many mine operators insisted on their services for a particularly harrowing journey up the mountain.

Although packers and freighters did their best, they could not keep up with the growing transport demands. At the same time, through no fault of their own, animals and wagons were proving too expensive and too slow. Rail access was needed to as many major supply towns in the San Juans as possible. In addition there were numerous potential mines that might be developed if a railroad could be brought close enough to move out the lower grade ore that they would produce. At first the railroads hesitated. The San Juans were a long way from Denver, and it cost an average of $25,000 to build one mile of track through the Colorado mountains – nearly half a million at today's prices. But when it became evident that the San Juan strike had the potential to continue for years, and even decades as some predicted, the railroads began pushing track towards southwestern Colorado.

The Denver and Rio Grande Railroad extended from Alamosa to Durango in 1881 and on to Silverton the following year. Freight that formerly cost $30.00 per ton to ship between Silverton and Durango by wagon dropped to $12.00 per ton by rail – and that was between Silverton and Denver. Large quantities of Silverton ore were sent to Durango for smelting or were processed in Silverton with high-quality coking coal shipped north from Durango to the Silverton smelters. A traveler was able to board the train in Silverton and, in relative comfort, be in Denver thirty hours later – a journey that previously took at least two weeks. The Denver and Rio Grande also reached Gunnison in late summer of 1881 and

Montrose less than a year after that. Track continued northward through the Uncompahgre Valley and on to Grand Junction and then towards Utah. By 1883 the San Juans were connected to both the east and west coasts by rails.

Meanwhile track construction continued into the San Juans. The general rule was that where profitable, ore could be hauled out and supplies hauled in, if rails were possible, they were laid. Ouray saw its first train in 1887, and tracks spread further into the San Juans. Otto Mears was quick to realize that these short-haul lines might be even more profitable than his toll roads, and he entered the railroad business with enthusiasm. Where the Denver and Rio Grande ended, Mears continued, pushing track deeper into the mountains. Without the funding available to established railroads, Mears was forced to borrow money. He sold construction bonds for six percent annual interest, payable every April and October in gold.

To reach the incredibly rich mines on Red Mountain between Silverton and Ouray, Mears built eighteen miles of track at a price almost twice the standard cost per mile of mountain rail. Nevertheless, the venture paid off handsomely as cars filled with rich ore moved down from Red Mountain towards Silverton. Mears continued to lay tracks north towards Ironton, a mere eight miles south of Ouray, but there he stopped. The vertical cliffs and grades proved impassable even for a narrow gauge train. Mears did not give up. If he could not connect Silverton to Ouray directly, he would find another route.

So began Otto Mears, Rio Grande Southern Railroad. More than 1000 men began laying track from Durango around and through the western end of the San Juans, working north. An additional 2,000 workers were spread across the route between Ridgway and Telluride. It was an incredible undertaking because Mears still had to traverse some of the most rugged country anywhere in the West. Graders, track layers, and thousands of horses and mules were used to blast and fill the new roadbed through mile after mile of mountain wilderness. Dozens of bridges had to be built. Then in 1891, the two construction crews met south of Telluride in Rico. A solid silver spike was driven into the last tie, dynamite blasts reverberated off the nearby mountainsides, and visiting bands (brought in by the new railroad) marched down Rico's main street playing their loudest. The saloons were filled to overflowing, and Otto Mears was proclaimed the hero of the day. Freight and passengers from almost anywhere in the San Juans were now

Digging out ahead of the train.
Courtesy Montrose County Historical Museum. Photo by Ben Walker.

thirty hours or less from Denver depending on weather and mechanical problems. However packers and wagon freighters continued to play an important role in the San Juans moving supplies and ore between the mines and the rails. Mules continued to be used as a source of transport in some mining operations as late as 1935.

Winter was the most unpredictable time for train travel in the San Juans. Deep snows and the resulting avalanches often cut off communities for weeks at a time. By February of 1884, the San Juans were so deep in snow that the train from Durango to Silverton did not run for seventy-three consecutive days. According to the March 15, 1884, issue of the *La Plata Miner,* snow was fifteen feet deep across Silverton's main street. The railroad fought back with gangs of shovelers. The trains of that day had no plows or blowers to remove snow from the track. It all had to be done by hand. Miners, unemployed for the winter, were hired in gangs of hundreds, and when necessary, they tunneled through an avalanche that had run across the tracks, often having to remove broken trees and boulders that had also been swept down the mountain. Otto Mears employed one hundred shovelers each winter just to keep the tracks clear over the eighteen-mile run between Silverton and Red Mountain. Fifty men would begin at each end of the line after a major snow, and they cleared track until the work teams met. Despite the best efforts of everyone involved, days and weeks sometimes passed when engines could not run because of deep snow. On occasion a train would become snowbound, but it was standard policy to carry two weeks' worth of emergency food and heating fuel during avalanche season.

Springtime brought flooding streams and rivers. More than one train crew plunged to their deaths as engines crashed through a bridge that had been weakened by high waters. The cycle of freezing and thawing shifted the

The Ophir Loop. Courtesy Montrose County Historical Museum.

rails, and spikes tended to pull loose from untreated and rotting wooden ties. These conditions led to frequent derailments. With the use of raw muscle and iron crowbars, train crews and passengers would lift the cars back onto the track and the journey would continue. In October of 1890 a train traveling from Silverton to Ironton derailed six times in four miles. In another incident near Silverton a loose rail tipped two cars over. One woman was thrown part way through an open window but only her hat was crushed. The cars were righted, and the train continued on its way. The lady was given a stiff drink–a standard procedure after an upset. The same accident crushed a box of peaches for which the railroad did reimburse the owner. It was official policy to pay only for damage to personal property. These and other troubles aside, it was the huffing, smoke-belching little narrow gauge mountain trains that allowed the San Juans to grow and prosper.

Rail travel also allowed for more than commercial transport. Trains brought circuses, theater-acting troupes, visiting family members and tourists. In 1888, the D.&R.G. began offering a tour of the San Juans that began in Denver, Colorado Springs, or Pueblo. Participants rode to Alamosa, from there to Chama, New Mexico, and then on to Durango and north to Silverton. At Silverton they changed trains and viewed the incredible beauty going up Red Mountain Pass, following much of present highway 550 and on to Ironton where they took a stage coach the final eight miles to Ouray. In Ouray they reboarded the D.&R. G. for Montrose, Gunnison, and then on back to their point of origin all for the cost of twenty-eight dollars. Thousands took advantage of the offer, making it very worthwhile for hotels and eating establishments along the route. The railroads themselves often carried dining cars that offered a variety of meals and imported alcoholic beverages designed to please even even the most discriminating diner. Fresh trout were often available when train crewmen threw sticks of dynamite into nearby creeks and then scooped up the fish stunned by the blast. For their own meals, crewmen fried steaks, potatoes and onions on coal shovels heated in the engine's fire box.

On special days trains ran from one town to another carrying loads of holiday revelers, bands, and baseball teams. Trains ran simply to allow passengers to look at the scenery or to pick wildflowers and hunt mushrooms. During the winter of 1887, the townspeople in Ouray took up a collection to buy hay for starving mountain sheep and elk that had come into town looking for food. The railroad obligingly hauled the fodder in at no cost to the town. Free travel passes were given to members of the clergy and other dignitaries. Otto Mears went so far as to give passes made of silver or even gold occasionally with a tiny inset diamond. Some of these can be seen in area museums today.

However it was the day-to-day commerce in freight and passengers that kept the San Juan railroads going. Hampered by difficult terrain, weather, and mechanical problems, they were not always on schedule, but they were a vital link between the region and the rest of the nation. By 1900 it cost a private shipper $2.05 to move one hundred pounds of freight from Chicago to Montrose by train. Twenty-five years earlier it would have cost that customer $3.50 to move the same freight fifty miles from Gunnison to Montrose.

Even so customers and passengers complained at times, especially about how slow mountain train travel could sometimes be. The Denver and Rio Grande Southern Railroad, which ran from Durango to Ridgway, bore more than its share of customer complaints and jokes. One story that was repeated for years in the Telluride area related to a verbal exchange between a very pregnant passenger and the conductor. The agitated woman demanded the train go faster as she was going into labor. The exasperated conductor told the lady that she should have had better sense than to have even gotten on the train in that condition. Her terse reply was that she had not been pregnant prior to boarding.

Chapter Four –
A Different Breed

In 1849 it took little more than determination, a bit of luck, and a metal pan to find and collect gold nuggets from the river sands and gravels of California. In the years that followed and as prospectors spread out across the American West, all that changed. The deposits of gold and silver they found were often in complex ores that took a great deal of knowledge to locate, extract, and process. The same proved true for those who came to southwestern Colorado to find and unlock the mineral secrets of the San Juans.

Unlike their predecessors, these prospectors often had technical backgrounds that enabled them to look for ores that would have been overlooked a decade or two earlier. In addition to their regular prospecting gear, many carried small arrays of laboratory equipment including chemicals such as hydrochloric and nitric acid. They were able to process, heat, and extract samples of complex ores on site. While most San Juan prospectors were not trained geologists, they were self-taught men who knew how to look for rock that might hold not only silver and gold but copper, lead, and mercury. Volcanic forces from ages past had left the San Juans with tortured and twisted masses of ore-bearing rock often deposited in ways that made their discovery extremely difficult. This problem was solved, in part, by the fact that gold and silver seekers came in large enough numbers to thoroughly explore the region. By 1880 more than 7,000 mining claims had been filed. As time progressed, and as the mountains gave up more and more of their secrets, new claims were filed on ore bodies that had previously escaped detection. For those engaged in the search for precious metals there was always the hope of finding riches that everyone else had missed, and sometimes they found them. When they did, the next step was to file on the ground involved and then put the claim up for sale. The actual process of mining the ore had to be left to those with the necessary capital to both open and operate a mine. Even a very promising claim sometimes pinched out a few feet below the surface and left the owner holding nothing of value. In other instances, claims that provided only mediocre assay results in the beginning sometimes led to incredible riches deeper into the rock.

The San Juans, throughout the mining years, proved many times that a potential ore body was pure speculation until it had actually been extracted and the money was in the bank.

Once a claim had been purchased, large expenditures had to be made before the first ounce of metal could be removed. A head works and other machinery to bring ore and waste rock up from below had to be built. In many instances, aerial trams were constructed to move ore down off the mountain. Shops, sorting rooms, ore bins, storage yards, and offices were also required. Steam engines and pumps had to be brought in and installed. Since most San Juan mines were too far from a town for an easy commute, living quarters had to be provided for up to 125 workers. A supply system had to be established to bring in food, coal, building materials, and mining equipment and to take ore back down the mountain. In some instances a mine came to resemble a small, self-contained town perched high on a mountain; indeed, that is exactly what it often became.

Only a portion of the mine employees actually mined. Vital to the entire operation was the company boarding house and dining hall. In some cases

Boarding houses were often owned and operated by women.
Courtesy Montrose County Historical Museum.

miners lived on site with their families in small, two room shacks, but generally, seventy-five percent of those on a mine's payroll were either single or living away from their families. Often, to save space and expense, one mine shift would use bunks in the boarding house, and when they went on shift, the off-going shift would climb into the beds vacated a short time earlier by their replacements – with the same bedding. Bigger mines did employ one or two young women to clean and tidy up. Even so, miners complained about the smells of a boarding house – a combination of cabbage, onions, tobacco smoke, stale grease, and a pungent collection of human body odors. In a few cases boarding houses were quite modern and designed with comfort and convenience in mind. The Camp Bird Mine southwest of Ouray provided its workers, after 1895, with indoor bathrooms fixtured with marble sinks, white enameled beds fitted with steel springs, modern mattresses, and an allocation of two men to a room (no sharing of beds).

Cooks were extremely important. Many times a good cook could be depended on to keep employees from seeking work at some other operation. If better prepared meals could be obtained elsewhere, men tended to change jobs. Consequently cooks were paid more than most of the men they fed. But they deserved it as they labored to feed individuals whose appetites were whetted by cold, high altitude, and hard work; yet these same conditions worked against the cook. Water boiled at a lower temperature at high altitudes, and it often took much longer to prepare a menu item. Beans were a particular problem, so they were boiled in large cans with tight fitting lids. The idea was to build up as much pressure inside as possible to hasten cooking time. Periodically the pressure would blow the lid off sending a spray of hot liquid and stray beans flying through the air. The lid was hammered back on, and the process repeated. Low atmospheric pressure caused yeast in rising bread to act abnormally fast, leaving large holes inside the loaf. That problem was combated by using extra salt to slow the rising process.

Breakfast was usually a combination of eggs, hotcakes, biscuits and gravy, and always some kind of meat. Biscuits were made with lard sometimes enough to constitute up to a third of this breakfast bread's weight. Coffee was also a perennial favorite in the high altitude mines, and because the coffee pots were continually in use they were seldom cleaned. One miner who had suffered through this problem later confided that the coffee was:

"much better adapted for staining floors or removing boiler scale." Breakfast over, the men who worked underground picked up lunches to take with them to eat mid-shift. These traditionally included a large bologna, egg, or ham sandwich; an apple, a piece of pie; and coffee or tea carried in the bottoms of sectioned but non-insulated metal lunch buckets. Miners ate again when they came off shift. A frequently prepared off-shift meal consisted of pinto beans, potatoes, and onions – all cooked together. A dessert of either pie, fruit cobbler, or a pudding was always expected. Bread and butter were standard staples. In some cases ethnic tastes were catered to. One popular menu item was Italian dumplings made with bread, milk, and flour, laced with chunks of salami and bacon, seasoned with parsley, and boiled in beef broth. Room and board were provided by the company but charged out at one dollar per day per man. Married men who lived in nearby company housing were charged rent which was deducted from their paychecks.

Activity was constant around a San Juan mine. Because of the extreme weather, as much work as possible was done inside the shelter of wooden buildings. Carpenters were usually busy at a mine site throughout the warmer months. Avalanches were frequent during the late winter and spring months, and many times buildings and structures that had been put up the previous year had to be repaired or replaced. Power was provided by steam engines which required a crew of men as well. In some cases coal was burned, but because of the high cost of getting coal up to the mine, wood was used whenever possible, and that involved cutting, collecting, and bringing it to the site. Boiler wood was cut into pieces five feet long. The logs then had to be split. While that process could be completed with a wedge and a maul, many boiler tenders preferred to bore a hole in one end, insert a quarter stick of dynamite, and blow the log apart. While easier, faster, and more entertaining for those involved, the process was dangerous. Another crew necessary at many mines were the 'cobbers.' Because of the expense of hauling ore down from the mountain, it was essential to first remove as much waste rock as possible. To do this, ore was taken into a building with high windows that let in adequate light, and older men, boys, or miners too injured to do any other work sorted the ore and broke away waste rock with a hammer. The remaining ore was then sacked and made ready for shipment. The waste rock was hauled to the mine dump. Cobbers were in danger of losing an eye now and then due to flying pieces of rock.

Because of the machinery, a certain number of mechanics or 'operating engineers,' were necessary. An above-ground crew that was of paramount importance were the men who worked in the blacksmith shop. Their primary job was to see to it that the miners had a steady supply of drills. These came in a wide selection of lengths, but they all had a cutting end that stood up to an average of fifteen minutes of work before it had to be resharpened. Tool runners would bring dulled drills to the blacksmith shop where they were heated red-hot, the chisel-shaped tip reformed, and then retempered by quenching in a tub of salt water. Blacksmiths also repaired or fabricated a variety of metal items and made machine parts. Generally their shops were equipped with the very latest of tools.

Mines provided their own signature of smells and sounds. There was wood smoke from the boilers and stoves mixed with the acrid odor of coking coal from the blacksmith shop. Signal bells clanged at the mine head, in conjunction with the whirring sound from the head frame sheaves as hoist cages or buckets were raised or lowered. At least twice a day there were dull rumbles coming from deep underground as explosives were detonated. Mules brayed as they were loaded with bags of ore, and there would be the sound of waste rock being unloaded at the mine dump. There was the squeak of wheels and pulleys from the aerial trams that lowered ore down the mountain. A nearby stamp mill might also add to the racket. Stamp mills often serviced several mines. An average facility took 300,000 board feet of lumber to build and 1,000 cubic yards of masonry to hold the 300 tons of machinery. A mill was powered by two boilers running a 200 horsepower steam engine which turned a cast iron flywheel nineteen feet in diameter. The object was to power a mechanism that raised and dropped several heavy cast iron stamps – some weighed up to 1,500 pounds each. Ore was crushed beneath the stamps to the consistency of sand. Then through the use of water, chemical, and mechanical means, most of the worthless rock was removed, and the concentrated ore was made ready for shipment to a smelter. In some instances the most complex concentrates were shipped all the way to England for final reduction. Stamp mills ran day and night. The thump, thump, thump reverberated through the earth itself. Both raw ore and ore concentrate were valuable enough to attract thieves, so there were always watchmen present even at the mines. These were often older men or employees unable to do heavy physical labor.

Routine, day-to-day operating expenses could be calculated and planned for by mine managers. But by far the most unpredictable expense was actually getting ore out of the ground. In 1880 it cost anywhere from $12.00 to $34.00 to drill and blast through six feet of rock. The figure varied according to the hardness of the material and whether the cut was horizontal, vertical, or somewhere in between. Ore bodies in the San Juans were unpredictable and would suddenly change direction or pinch out and then continue at some point deeper inside the mountain. To know where to drill and blast took the expertise of a mine supervisor. Most men who filled this position were college graduates with practical experience in Mexico or South America. It was their responsibility to decide where to tunnel or dig. A good superintendent was said to be a man who 'had a nose for ore.' He worked very closely with underground supervisory personnel, constantly watching for clues as to where a particular vein or ore body might be going. The idea was to avoid removing any more rock than necessary. In mines where profits were slim, a few incorrect calls by the superintendent might well take an operation into bankruptcy. However he was not the only person upon whose shoulders rode the financial fortunes of owners and stockholders. Above ground the company assayer bore his share of responsibility.

From a scientific standpoint, a late nineteenth century assayer was ahead of even the doctors of his time. It was he who subjected samples of ore to analysis that used both chemicals and fire to determine the precious metal content. In the San Juans he had to contend with ores that contained not only gold and silver, but lead, copper, and other trace minerals as well. By sampling a few ounces of ore, an assayer had to be able to accurately determine how many ounces of precious metal an entire ton of that ore contained. Fortunes rode on those determinations. Appropriately enough, most assayers were considered on the same social level as bankers and mine superintendents. They usually worked in a three-room office. The office portion was in front where samples were received, paperwork done, and visits with the superintendent and other mine officials conducted. The middle room was a laboratory, and it was kept clean, tidy, and as dust free as possible. The back room was for storage, and it was there that an apprentice crushed ore samples. A typical assay involved taking exactly two ounces of crushed ore and placing it in a crucible which was heated to 1,500 degrees

Centigrade. After thirty minutes the melted sample was poured into a receiving vessel, cooled, the slag broken away, and the remaining button of precious metal subjected to a second heating. This time the goal was to flux off all metals other than gold and silver. If the temperature was allowed to go a few degrees one way or the other, the sample was ruined as far as determining precisely how much silver and gold it contained. Once an assayer was certain he had nothing but precious metal remaining, the material was cooled again and weighed on a very sensitive balance scale. The tiny button of gold and silver was then treated with acid to dissolve the silver until only the gold remained. After the fragment of gold was weighed, the assayer could determine how much silver had been dissolved away. By constantly measuring the richness of ore that came out of a mine each day, the superintendent could determine where to drill and blast. Mine management's knowledge about the value of each day's production also helped keep concentrating mills and smelters reasonably honest. A skilled assayer was a man in demand. The very best had been trained in England, but, for most practitioners of the business, they learned their trade through long and arduous apprenticeships.

Never far from the assayer were owners and stockholders. Hotels in nearby towns were often filled with those who had financial interests in San Juan mines. They came and went; trips were part vacation and part business. Dividends were high; sometimes as much as forty-five percent of annual profits were paid per share of stock. From the early 1870s until 1893 it was silver that made San Juan fortunes. Copper, lead, zinc, and small quantities of gold were also extracted, and these metals played a role in determining profits. But it was value of silver that determined whether a mine was successful or not.

Lead-based ores could be smelted in either Silverton or Durango, but copper-based ore had to be transported by rail to either Pueblo or Denver for processing. This extra cost sometimes determined whether a mine could remain profitable or not. As margins narrowed, mine operators responded by continuing to increase production. By 1885 Ouray's mineral output was surpassed only by Leadville and Aspen, a fact mentioned at different times by Ouray's three newspapers. In 1886 the mines on Red Mountain, south of Ouray, shipped an estimated 15,100 tons of ore. In 1890 those same mines produced in excess of 20,000 tons of ore but production costs continued to rise. The deeper the Red Mountain mines went, the more water they had to contend with, in addition to the fact that deeper ores were often not as rich as those closer to the surface. The Guston Mine was at 1,300 feet, the Yankee Girl was more than 1,000 feet below the surface, and other mines were not far behind. Operators were forced to bring in, at tremendous cost, bigger and more powerful pumps to keep the acid-rich waters from flooding the diggings. Despite silver ore that yielded from 100 to 450 ounces of silver per ton (occasional pockets produced as much as 15,000 ounces per ton), profit margins continued to depend largely on the volume of ore produced. To help keep costs in line, recycling was practiced on a grand scale. If a mine brought in new machinery, neighboring operations quickly snapped up the older machines – particularly engines, boilers, and pumps – for their own use. Fires and avalanches also cut into profits. Although property insurance was available, it seldom covered more than twenty percent of the on-site assets. Owners were liable for the remainder. Still, with a bit of luck, a certain degree of shrewdness, and if a mine was operated properly, fortunes could be made in spite of high production costs. But first there had to be a mine.

Mining claims and working mines constantly changed owners. Claims were often bought and held purely for speculative purposes. Some changed hands numerous times but never were developed. Working mines were also frequently sold, and most owners felt their properties were worth more than they actually were. After all there was always the chance (and it did happen on numerous occasions) that new owners would drill and blast a few feet and discover vastly richer ore. Sometimes, however, sellers would whet the appetite of a potential buyer by creating the illusion that an ore body was richer than it actually was. The process was called "salting." Earlier western miners had been known to fire a shotgun loaded with gold dust into a rock face to make it appear richer. By San Juan days, such crude efforts would have been laughed at.

Potential buyers would bring in their own mining engineers who would examine a digging and then watch carefully as the face was drilled, explosives installed, and ore blasted out. Still under careful supervision, that ore would be taken to the surface and brought directly to an assayer. Some engineers insisted on a second drilling and blasting just in case the first layer of rock might have been tampered with. In other instances cheaters would attempt to add rich pieces of ore they had hidden, either in the mine or inside their clothing, to the freshly blasted rock. More commonly they attempted to select the very best pieces of ore that had been blasted loose, but a good supervising engineer was wise to such tricks. A sizable percentage of San Juan mines also contained a few ounces of gold per ton of ore, which increased the profit margin. So it was to gold that the potential salters usually turned their attention. It only took a tiny amount to influence an ore sample. Schemers learned to inject gold dust into sticks of dynamite, and then use those explosives right under the noses of the examining engineers. A more certain method involved secretly injecting liquid gold chloride into the sealed sample bags before they reached the assayer. This was a tricky procedure because if it wasn't done exactly right, the assayer would be suspicious. To prevent such chicanery, the men involved would be carefully searched for syringes or other similar devices. In at least one instance a man drank a gold chloride solution, and with careful timing, managed to secretly urinate in the ore samples before they reached the assayer. His efforts were not successful.

A more common problem for mine owners involved their own workers. For days or weeks a crew might drill and blast and remove the ore and then suddenly discover a pocket of exceptionally rich ore sometimes almost pure silver and gold. If the shift boss was not looking (and sometimes when he was), the drillers would secrete a few pieces of the metal in the bottoms of their lunch buckets, in their pockets, or even under their hats. The process was known as 'high grading.' To combat such thievery, lunch buckets were often searched, and miners were forced to change and leave their working clothes at the mine all this under the watchful eyes of a supervisor. However no matter what was done, high grading was a fact of mining. Resourceful high graders would sometimes hide small pieces of ore in a false crown inside the hats they wore. Muckers and anyone directly involved in moving the ore up out of the mine could try their hand at filching a few pieces of ore when the occasion arose. Once outside the mine the opportunity increased each time the ore was handled or stored. It only took half a teaspoon of gold to equal ten dollars more than three days' pay for the average miner. High grading also occurred in the concentrating mills. Mill employees routinely stole small amounts of concentrated ore and then sold it to individuals who, in turn, found markets for it with various smelters. On a less serious side, zinc concentrate was routinely high-graded by mill employees to take home and throw into their heating stoves. The resulting reaction helped clean soot out of the stove pipes. Most men did not consider what they were doing as actually stealing. They frequently felt that they were being underpaid by mine owners, and rich eastern stockholders and few were concerned that a jury of peers could ever be found to convict them. Generally, if caught, high graders were simply fired. It was of no great concern because they could find another job further down the road.

There were other, less controllable risks that miners took. Three out of four men who labored in the San Juans were either single or had left their families back East or in Europe. If they were injured or sick, they had to depend on others to care for them. For this reason most of the early hospitals built in the region were primarily for sick or injured miners without families. The bigger mining concerns deducted one dollar per month from each employee's pay and contracted with either a local physician or hospital or both to care for injuries or illnesses. In some cases this insurance was available for the families of married men. Railroad workers had the same form of insurance plan and for the same cost. The actual benefits of such programs often depended on the skills and dedication of the contracting physicians.

Veteran miners usually had at least a partial awareness about the health and injury risks involved with their work, but the influx of newcomers seldom did. Experienced men tended to gravitate to mines with a better safety or health record. New immigrants were left to work in the more dangerous operations until they too gained enough experience to move on, but often, for many, it would be too late. Sharp particles of rock dust would already be eating away at their lungs. The condition would eventually prove either crippling or fatal. Accidents caused by ignorance or inexperience claimed arms, legs, and eyes, as well as lives. There was no compensation in such cases. The U.S. courts of the time had ruled that a man chose to work by his own free will and thus was due no extra compensation from his employer in cases of injury or death. Management often took advantage of the ruling and cut corners to save money, many times at risk to the employees. Safety features inside the mines were often never installed. For lack of simple board barricades, men stepped into open underground shafts and fell screaming to their deaths. Steam boilers were allowed to rust to the point that they became dangerous. Boiler explosions were common. Mill and smelter workers sickened from exposure to the mercury that was used to extract gold. Coal miners in the Durango area were paid only for the coal they produced, not for the necessary shoring they had to do to keep the tunnels from collapsing. Sometimes, in the interest of saving time, they failed to shore properly and paid with their lives for their haste. Then there were the smelter workers in the Telluride area who worked with ores that contained sulfur and selenium. While these men did not exhibit any visible signs of illness, passersby had only to catch a whiff of their fetid breath to know that they were smelter workers.

Weather claimed its share of victims as well. Men going on or off shift sometimes lost their way in blinding storms and died of exposure. In 1898 the foreman of the Humboldt Mine above Telluride accidentally walked off the edge of a 500 foot cliff in a blinding snow storm and plunged to his death. More directly there was the danger of avalanches. Many mines were located at or near timberline and often in the path of avalanche runs, although this was sometimes not known until men and buildings were swept away in a roar of ice and snow. Mines could not be moved, so efforts were made to either minimize avalanche danger or deflect it in some way. This seldom proved effective. A boarding house in Ironton Park south of Ouray was built with a roof four feet thick and designed to deflect the snow and ice over the top. In 1899 a slide occurred, and the boarding house suffered only slight damage. Sometime later another one struck and this time, swept the entire structure down the mountain. Perhaps the worst avalanche occurred at the Liberty Bell Mine near Telluride on March 1, 1902. The first torrent of ice and snow swept away part of the buildings killing and burying the inhabitants. A rescue party quickly reached the site of the disaster only to be swept to their own deaths in a second slide. Nineteen individuals lost their lives that day.

A fact that presents itself over and over is the selflessness of those who were willing to risk their lives on such missions of mercy. One of the best known stories involved a young miner from Ouray named Billy Maher who was badly injured in a dynamite explosion near the Virginius Mine in February of 1891. Four Virginius miners placed Maher on a sled and began the journey down to Ouray through deep snow and during a blinding storm. Word was sent ahead for a relief crew from another mine to meet them half

Winter in the high San Juans.
Courtesy Montrose County Historical Museum. Photo by Ben Walker.

way. The exhausted Virginius men reached the rendezvous point but found no relief crew. Valiantly they pushed ahead through the strengthening storm. They were almost past the point of human endurance when they reached the Ouray hospital but it was too late for young Billy Maher. The effects of the explosion and the trek down the mountain had proven too much and he died a few hours later. His rescuers rested that night and then began their journey back to the Virginius, angry and eager for a confrontation with those who had failed to meet and assist them the day before. They were not quite half way when they met other searchers and learned that the relief party had been on its way to meet them only to be swept to their deaths in another avalanche.

But, storms ended, snows melted, and optimism returned for those who lived and worked in the San Juans. A variety of fraternal lodges populated every mining town and provided men with a place to visit, play cards or billiards, and sometimes the opportunity to look for a better job. The Independent Order of Odd Fellows, Knights of Columbus, Knights of Pythias, Ancient Order of Hibernians, The International Order of

Woodsmen of the World, and the Benevolent and Protective Order of Elks were some of the better known fraternal groups. For many single miners, a lodge was a substitute for family. Here was a circle of ready-made friends, and an environment away from the mine and street where a man could relax and enjoy himself. Lodges also sponsored their members in various mining contests particularly those held on the Fourth of July. Most had elaborate uniforms they proudly wore in parades, and some even provided semi-military drill teams complete with rifles and swords. Most lodge members proudly displayed their particular affiliation by wearing the lodge insignia, dangling free at the the end of a watch chain. If a lodge member moved to another town or camp, he found instant acceptance among lodge brothers of that area. Many fraternal societies offered their own life insurance to miners that was often cheaper than traditional companies offered at the time. Some provided burial insurance and even tombstones.

In addition to lodges there were clubs and other groups for interested miners and townsmen alike. Bands were popular. Silverton had a marching band in the 1880s that gained national renown when it played at President Harrison's inauguration in Washington. By the late 1880s baseball had become a national passion, and the San Juan mining towns proved no exception. Each had its own team, and rivalry was intense as the champions of one town team were pitted against those of another. Frequently an entire train would be chartered to transport both team and fans to a game in a rival town. In a more serious vein, labor unions began to make their presence felt in the San Juan camps by the late 1880s. They too had a recreational side. The Knights of Labor sponsored fancy balls and frequent dances played for by local bands. The Knights of Labor also furnished and underwrote the costs of maintaining libraries and public reading rooms in various towns. Local newspapers were widely read. During the cold winters, when large numbers of men were unemployed, debating societies were popular. In 1874 the Silverton Debating Society sponsored the debate: "Resolved that a burro has no right that a miner is bound to respect." The event was well attended, and the side that chose to support burro rights lost.

A high percentage of the single San Juaners had served, on one side or the other, in the Civil War. They were part of a transient population attracted to mining, railroad building, construction, and lumbering and they often hitched rides on freight trains although most considered themselves several cuts above traditional hoboes. While they were good workers, their penchant for change made them more mobile than their married brothers. When a miner decided it was time to quit his job and move on, he would tell his companions that "the hole is deep enough," and he would be off to new places. But there was also a sense of universalness to the experiences these men shared. Most were under thirty-five, the majority liked to drink, and a high percentage were interested in sex; 'amatory recreation' they called it. The flesh trade was an integral part of most mining communities.

Practical jokes were endemic among the mining crowd and were often played out on an elaborate scale particularly for the uninitiated newcomer. At a cabin south of Ouray, the two inhabitants invited several acquaintances over for an evening of card playing. During the course of the game the two hosts began showing signs of hostility towards each other until finally, after one accused the other of cheating, both drew pistols. The lone candle on the table was snuffed out, and rounds of gunfire were punctuated by angry curses. In terror for their lives, the other participants trampled each other attempting to gain passage through the outside door. Moments into the drama the gunfire ceased, and the curses were replaced with shrieks of laughter a situation that only helped to confound the innocent bystanders outside in the snow. When the candle was finally relit they were greeted by their two hosts who had set the whole thing up and had loaded their pistols with blanks. Everyone eventually agreed it had been a splendid joke, and the game was resumed. Generally the mining crowd settled differences with fists, and in some cases, with knives the latter, usually in a state of extreme inebriation. When firearms were used to settle a grudge, it was usually a pimp ambushing a competitor in a dark alley.

Cards, or "pasteboards," as they were referred to, were generally an innocent form of recreation. Men would sit for hours, each with a cheek full of plug tobacco that went by names like Granger's Twist, Star, Horseshoe and Piper Heidsick the latter heavily laced with licorice. In polite company players periodically directed streams of tobacco juice towards the nearest spittoon or against a hot stove. In saloons and gaming houses they often spit on the floor. Gambling came with its own risks. One Ouray miner who sold his share of a rich mining claim for $20,000 became addicted to gaming houses and the faro tables. Within a short time he had lost his entire fortune and was forced to go back to work as a common mine laborer. It was not unusual for a man who found himself in such straits to end his life by going off alone and blowing himself up with dynamite.

For the more prudent, there were less expensive forms of recreation. Most San Juan towns were home to a variety of eating establishments, and to provide a change from boarding house food, men liked to eat out. Until 1935 mining was a seven day a week occupation with payday every other Saturday. Often on payday night miners would don their blue serge suits and cock a Derby hat rakishly over one eye, and eat out at one of the very best places in town. The Sheridan Hotel dining room in Telluride was a favorite of miners in that area. The menu was in French, and it became a standard joke to suggest to the uninitiated that they try the last item on the menu which happened to be the chef's name. To lend depth to the jest, waiters would solemnly pronounce that the item in question was not available. After a fine meal the dining party would depart to spend the remainder of the evening at their lodge, in one of the many saloons or dance halls or perhaps to seek a bit of amatory affection at one of the many houses that plied that particular trade.

The mining companies, all too aware of some of the moral and financial pitfalls that lurked in the towns on payday night, frequently sponsored company dances right at the mine. Carefully chaperoned and providing free food, these events were opportunities for the respectable girls and women from the town, and nearby farms and ranches to enjoy an evening out. It was not unusual for female participants to travel most of a day to attend. Lodges and various civic groups also sponsored community dances. These too were low-key and kept quite respectable. The females at most dances were usually married, and it was considered proper for them to dance with anyone who asked. A majority of the respectable girls were married by age fifteen, so potential single partners were usually in the minority.

For the upper crust of the mining hierarchy who chose to entertain the fair sex, there were the hotel lobbies. Young mining engineers were frequently seen in the company of single female school teachers reciting poetry, reading aloud to each other, or singing. It was a respectable way to court in a society where private homes were not always available, and it prevented scandal for the young women involved. Few early San Juan school teachers were ever employed more than one year before they were married and settled into housekeeping – much to the consternation of local school boards.

Most days and nights were an established routine of work, eat, and sleep for the majority of San Juan miners. Some made use of their free hours by studying subjects that would advance them up the employment ladder. From 1875 until past the turn of the century, the San Juans led the world in mining technology. Mines that used alternating electric current to run their pumps and motors, ore concentration facilities, and smelting operations all needed men who were willing to advance their technical backgrounds.

The San Juan mining camps did get together to celebrate one major holiday each year – the Fourth of July. Mines closed for three days, and nearly everyone made their way to the towns of Silverton, Durango, Telluride, Ouray, and Lake City. There were parades with marching bands and all the lodges were represented with their members decked out in quasi-military uniforms trimmed with gold and silver braid. Volunteer fire departments put on demonstrations and participated in hose cart races. There were mining contests involving speed and skill. Men competed to see who could shovel a ton of ore into an ore cart in the least amount of time. Champion drilling teams represented the mines in the area, and the two men who could drill the deepest hole in a slab of granite in fifteen minutes received up to one thousand dollars in prize money. Side bets by the observers totaled many thousands more. There were also boxing matches. These were fought without benefit of gloves and ended when a man was knocked out or could not get up. There were horse and mule races. Throughout the holiday dynamite explosions echoed off the surrounding mountain sides. Beer was dispensed by the wagon load. Kids had their own events involving foot, sack and burro races which sometimes, to the delight of the spectators, were more rodeo events than races. The evenings were devoted to community dances, and, in addition to prodigious amounts of food available throughout the day, there was also a community supper at midnight and then dancing until dawn for those with the constitution for it. Native born and immigrant all celebrated the holiday with equal enthusiasm.

The second major holiday celebrated in the San Juans was Christmas, but it was a quiet time. Families celebrated at home. Church services were well attended. Midnight Catholic masses, from surviving accounts, attracted Catholics and Protestants alike. The saloons were decorated and the piano player ran through his repertoire of Christmas carols. Cornish miners assembled impromptu choirs and serenaded the town with Christmas hymns. With up to seventy-five percent of the area's population either single or away from their families, Christmas was frequently a painful holiday, heavy with memories and longings. The houses of ill-repute, from the fanciest parlor houses to the lowest cribs, all closed on Christmas Eve and remained closed for Christmas Day. Suicides were more common during the Christmas season than any other time of the year.

Most San Juaners came to southwestern Colorado in hopes of making money — hopefully lots of money. Their business was mining, and directly or indirectly, nearly everyone was tied to the metals that lay hidden beneath the jagged peaks of the San Juans. From shopkeepers and freighters to saloon owners and parlor house madams, everyone depended on the men who willingly went underground each day to drill, blast and retrieve the glittering tons of ore rich in silver, gold, copper, lead, and zinc.

CHAPTER FIVE –
At the Mine

The winter night sky was still enveloped in an inky blackness that accentuated the light from the unwavering stars above. A steam whistle pierced the predawn darkness. It was 6:00 a.m., and for those not already up, the shrill scream was a warning that work was an hour away. In company bunkhouses and private shacks, men had already rolled out of bed wearing two-piece woolen undergarments with long legs and short sleeves. The front of the undershirt opened wide enough so that a man could slip both his head and arms through and wear the garment around his waist while he was working. Over his underwear went a heavy pull-over shirt and trousers that came only to his ankles, so that they would not drag through muck and water. Socks were heavy wool, and in many cases, men wore only strips of flour sacks wound round and round the foot and ankle – how many wraps depended on the particular situation. Shoes came in whole sizes from six to twelve. A few individuals, mostly supervisors and engineers, wore boots, while the rank and file favored ankle-high, square-toed brogan style shoes smeared with marmot fat to protect the leather from wet rock floors. The soles were double thick and had rows of hob nails driven into the bottoms to resist wear on the sharp, abrasive rocks inside the mines.

Breakfast was wolfed down, newly packed lunch buckets picked up, and during the cold months, a man bundled himself into a heavy fleece Mackinaw coat to wear to and from the mine. Most men who worked underground wore a thick, felt hat heavily smeared with resin or painted with linseed oil to stiffen it. These provided a limited amount of protection from bumps and falling rocks. The morning crews checked in at the mine head by seven o'clock.

If a man worked in a "wet mine" (and many of the San Juan mines fell into this category) he removed his outer clothes and changed into another set still wet and clammy from when he had peeled out of them at the end of his previous shift twelve hours earlier. Next he picked up whatever tools and supplies he needed. The night crew, coming off their shift, would have set off charges of explosives before leaving the work area. Time was needed to help clear the mine of blasting fumes and dust. All told, a man working a ten-hour shift was actually at the mine for twelve. One hour was taken to go on and off shift with another hour typically allowed for lunch, noon or midnight as the case might be. Some miners were only allowed thirty minutes to eat. Work weeks were a minimum of six days with seven being common during busy periods.

The National Bell Mine. Courtesy Montrose County Historical Museum.

The mine employees at a typical San Juan mine numbered from a few dozen up to 125, and they worked a variety of jobs. The drillers were the men who were best known, because it was they who actually engaged in the work of extracting ore. After changing clothes and picking up tools and supplies they made their way down elevators and through narrow, twisting tunnels to their work areas. Each man was issued three or four high-quality candles prior to his shift. These would be carried in simple iron holders that could be wedged into the rock near the work area. In the case of breezy or drafty tunnels, the candles would be carried in shielded lanterns. Sometimes oil lanterns were used. By 1890 electric lights were common in many of the bigger San Juan mines. Carbide lights were not introduced until ten years after that.

Muckers would already be at work shoveling away ore and waste rock that had been blasted loose on the previous shift. The shift boss made an inspection of the face area for any explosives that might not have detonated and once satisfied, would inscribe chalk marks where he wanted new holes drilled. He had to be able to determine which way the vein of mineral was going. Once that chore was completed, the miners took their places and began the tedious task of drilling holes. Before the days of steam and air-powered drills, this was accomplished by hand. If the face had limited working space, then holes were cut by a process known as "single jacking." With a long handled steel drill, the tip shaped similar to a chisel, a miner would attack a chalk mark with a four pound hammer. Between blows he would rotate the drill a few degrees to keep it from binding and to keep the hole round. After six inches of cutting the now dulled drill would be exchanged for a fresh one several inches longer. The process was repeated at six inch intervals until the hole was thirty inches deep. Often when a vein was too narrow to allow for much more than crawl room, single jacking was the only way to extract the ore without removing too much waste rock. Miners called this method "rat holing."

Where space allowed for more working room, holes could be cut by a faster process known as "double jacking." In this instance one miner held the drill and rotated it, while his partner swung an eight pound sledge hammer at fifty strokes per minute. Periodically the two would exchange places. The process was carried out in nothing more than the dim flicker of candle light. One missed blow by a eight pound hammer could shatter the forearm or hand of the man holding the drill. Sweat poured out, and shirts and undershirts were pulled down around the men's waists. Drillers in the San Juan mines were often experienced miners who had come from the tin mines in Cornwall, England. Cornish miners were extremely fraternal. If a drilling job opened up they almost always seemed to know of another Cornish miner who could be called in. Many times he was said to be a cousin, and "Jack" was a popular name among these English immigrants. So it was that Cornish miners came to be known by others as "Cousin Jacks." Mining was their life, and proud of their skills, they counted themselves among the elite of American mine workers. They brought with them their superstitions, their customs, and beautiful acappella voices which they used at funerals and Christmastime. They even brought their favorite foods.

Lunch for a Cornish miner was preferably a "pasty" (rhymes with blasty). It was a piece of thick dough folded over a filling of chopped beef or pork, onions, turnips, and potatoes and then salted, peppered and baked. Cornish men, mostly single and living in company boarding houses, were particular about who made this delicacy. They believed it took a woman's touch and if one was not available they would sometimes make trouble with the male cooks who failed to chop the meat or vegetables properly. They insisted on their tea as well. Miners carried round lunch pails that came apart in sections. The bottom part was designed to contain liquids. Three nails were driven into a board to serve as a stand for the lunch bucket and a lighted candle stub was placed underneath stubs left over from the previous day. The process was timed to have the tea warm by lunch. Other miners adopted the same process for coffee. But above all, the Cornish were noted for their work ethic. The sound of hammers against steel drills was the song they sang in the mines.

Shift bosses stopped by periodically to make sure the work was going smoothly. As the hours passed, boys who were twelve or thirteen years old

An early blacksmith shop. Courtesy Ouray County Historical Society.

would drop off armloads of freshly sharpened drills and remove the dulled ones for a trip to the blacksmith shop to be resharpened. These young tool runners were also responsible for bringing and removing candle boxes partially filled with dirt. These were used for latrines. In bigger mines a special ore car was painted red and fitted with a two or three-hole seat. These "potty wagons" would then be periodically hoisted to the surface and dumped.

Not only was drilling hard work, but it became complicated when ore bodies twisted, pinched and sometimes traveled upwards. In these cases drillers had to work above their heads. Swinging an eight pound hammer in direct opposition to gravity was an almost super-human task, and the men had no way to shield their eyes from flying rock chips. In this situation the ceiling was unsupported by shoring timbers, and rock falls were frequent and sometimes fatal. Other dangers lurked as well. Although ventilation tunnels were used whenever possible, blasting fumes, particularly those of dynamite, often lingered well into a new shift and caused headaches and burning eyes. Neither condition was beneficial to the man holding the drill or to his partner swinging the hammer.

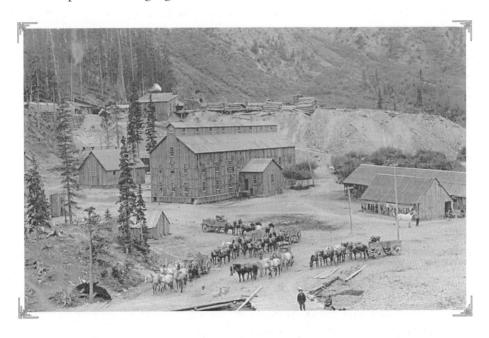

The Revenue Mine complex - 1896. Courtesy Ouray County Historical Society.

A few of the bigger mines could afford to use steam drills which were introduced shortly after the Civil War, and they were much faster than drill and hammer. Miners aptly named them "widow makers." The problem was that as they cut into the rock they made dust. Tiny fragments of silica rock, sharp as razors, filled the air and were breathed into the lungs of those present. First came a wracking cough, and, depending on amount of exposure, within months or a few years at best, the victim would be slowly incapacitated with what was known asz"miner's consumption." Corrosive chemicals released in the same dust also ate through the victim's lungs and throat lining. Death was by slow and painful suffocation. Autopsies showed lung tissue so scarred that it was almost petrified. Most San Juan miners exposed to silica dust were dead by the age of forty. Steam-powered drills were also prone to broken lines resulting in scalding burns and, on occasion, would blow up in the hands of the operator. As technology improved, they were replaced with drills powered by compressed air, but it was not until 1900 that a feature was incorporated to inject water into the drill tip so as to end the dust problem.

Once all the holes were cut, all tools and personal items would be picked up, counted, and removed to a safe location. A long handled wooden or copper rod with a spoon-like scoop on the end would be used to clean remaining debris from each hole, and then the explosives would be inserted. During the early years paper tubes of black powder were used to which were attached long fuses that extended out from the hole and down the face for a predetermined distance. The holes were then carefully filled with either rock cuttings or damp clay to help direct the blast into the rock. After 1875 black powder was replaced by dynamite. This was a mixture of nitroglycerine and either sawdust or special clays. It was up to five times more powerful than black blasting powder and could prove many times more dangerous. Early San Juaners called it "giant powder." Dynamite came in sticks of thirty, forty, or sixty percent strength and normally was very stable. Detonation was accomplished by attaching a small metal cartridge containing fulminate-of-mercury which detonated the dynamite stick as the blasting cartridge itself was detonated by a length of Bickford fuse. The fuse had to be inserted into the open end of the detonator and then crimped. It only took a small amount of mechanical force to explode the fulminate-of-mercury. Some miners used their teeth to crimp the fuse into the blasting cartridge rather than use the special crimping tool provided, sometimes with fatal results. If a blasting cartridge went off in a man's hand he could expect to lose several fingers, but that was better than half his face. Bickford fuse consisted of six strands of jute which were machine wrapped around a core of black powder and sealed with a waterproof tape. It had a burn rate of one foot every thirty seconds and was generally reliable, but occasions did occur when it proved defective and would almost cease to burn. The jute would continue to glow, and this smoldering spark might travel slowly to the next viable portion of fuse which would suddenly sputter back to life. Sometimes this process could consume minutes or even hours, and a man risked his mortal life to reenter an area where a charge had failed to go off. Although electrical blasting was available as early as 1871, San Juan miners continued to use fuse and blasting cartridges well into the twentieth century. On occasion a stick of unexploded dynamite would go undetected by the oncoming shift. If the drill of an unsuspecting miner punched into the sensitive blasting cap, the results would be similar to standing in front of an exploding cannon. After such an accident the walls of the working area were coated with quicklime to neutralize the smell of burned flesh and blood.

Ouray miners in a blacksmith shop. Courtesy Ouray County Historical Society.

But most detonations were routine, and once everything was in readiness, the fuses were lit and the crew made an orderly retreat to a safe area. The crew boss would count each blast, and any he failed to detect would be reported to the oncoming crew of the next shift. A properly fired round would remove about thirty-two tons of ore and rock and advance the hole or heading by another three feet.

It was the job of the muckers to remove ore and rock. Mucking was usually the first job a man was given when he went to work in a San Juan mine, and at the time, because of a heavy influx of Irish immigrants, many muckers were of that nationality. Ore was scooped into wheelbarrows (nicknamed Irish buggies), and then moved either to an ore car on rails or directly to the shaft to be dumped into a hoisting bucket. In some cases it was dumped into ore chutes, which periodically were emptied into the hoisting buckets that took the ore to the surface. Mucking was backbreaking work and multiple hernias or ruptured spinal disks were common. In the case of hernias a sufferer bound the affected area in a truss that would keep the injury stable. In the situation of a badly injured spinal disk, a man was through with mining. Although the work was brutal, most Irish muckers believed they had a better life than the one they had left behind in Europe. In Ireland a man could still be arrested, tried, and sent to the penal colonies of Australia for poaching a rabbit on public land. At that time most Irish could afford to eat meat only at Christmas and Easter and lived on buttermilk and potatoes the remainder of the year. In the San Juans a man could eat meat every day with the hope that his children would do even better.

Numerous nationalities were represented in the mountains of southwestern Colorado. In addition to the Cornish and the Irish there were Italians, Germans, Eastern Europeans, Greeks, and native-born Americans who came from both the North and the recently vanquished former states of the Confederacy. Many times only half the workers in a mine spoke English. For this reason a mining vocabulary was developed that, while understandable to those involved, often left visitors completely dumbfounded. Because of the nature of mining, miners also developed a fraternal relationship with their fellow workers. One retired Irish miner, interviewed in his nineties, had this to say about that time: "all those nationalities, creeds and colors. They worked together, danced together, and sometimes fought. But they didn't fight much."

The Cornish drilled and blasted. The Irish and the Italians mucked, but the mines could not run with these two occupations alone. Hoist operators worked the buckets, cages, or lifts that moved ore up out of the mine. Cage tenders were responsible for getting ore cars loaded onto the hoists, and top loaders emptied those cars once they reached the surface. Powder men were responsible for storing and issuing explosives. Pump men took care of the big bronze-lined pumps that lifted water out of the shafts and kept the mines from flooding. Engineers ran the boilers that powered the pumps and drills. Timber men brought in and installed the shoring timbers eight feet long and eight inches by eight inches. Construction carpenters on a grand scale, these men were specialists who knew how to place and install the vital shoring that kept mines from collapsing under the tremendous forces exerted by the mountains above. Their boss was the timber foreman, and he generally made decisions regarding pumping, inter-mine transportation, and mine animals, if they were used. With special exceptions, these were the individuals directly involved in sub-surface operations.

In addition to the activities of drilling, mucking, and timbering, mines were scenes of other activities as well. A considerable amount of building and repair (done by the timber men) was always in progress. Mines had elaborate infrastructures made of wood, and these structures had to be replaced periodically. Nails and bolts rusted away quickly. Water leaching through the rock in many San Juan mines turned into a weak solution of sulfuric acid which quickly ate away at anything made of iron or steel. Mines in the Red Mountain area between Silverton and Ouray were especially prone to this phenomenon, and sulfuric acid levels were so high that pump pipes corroded out and had to be replaced as often as every two weeks. The braided, flat wire cable used to hoist buckets and cages up and down the shafts was particularly vulnerable to acid corrosion. These and other machine parts were kept coated with grease, a messy and never-ending job.

To remove the water that perpetually seeped into the mines, huge pumps were used. These monsters cycled six to seven times per minute, each upstroke lifting nearly a ton of mud, arsenic, and sulfide-tainted water. The pumps themselves weighed several tons and were lined with bronze to help prevent corrosion. A large one could cost as much as $30,000 in a time when a mansion could be built for less than $5,000. Pump men had to be unceasingly vigilant in case a pump rod broke. If this occurred, the operator had only seconds to shut the machinery down, or the water coming up the shaft would begin to flow backwards and the weight would cause the pump to rapidly pick up speed and disintegrate. Without the pumping operation going twenty-four hours a day, water would quickly flood the working level of the mine. Even on holidays the pumps continued to run.

The rates at which miners were paid depended on what they did. Wages were fairly constant from 1870 until 1900. Drillers averaged three to three and a half dollars per shift. Muckers, timber men, and other underground workers received from two dollars and fifty cents to three dollars for the same period. Technicians who operated the pumps, boilers and hoists got four dollars. Shift bosses and other supervisory personnel were paid five dollars per day. The mine superintendent received a monthly salary that averaged three hundred dollars.

A winter pack train. Courtesy Ouray County Historical Society. Photo by Ben Walker.

The shift boss, usually working in cooperation with the timber foreman, was in charge underground. His word was law, and he could fire a man in an instant. Drinking on the job was not tolerated. Still, in a time when alcoholism was rampant among miners, some were willing to take the chance, because often another job could be had in another mine a few miles away. In a related but harder to detect situation, muckers and timber men frequently took opiates for chronic back pain. Narcotic-dulled muckers sometimes forgot to stop at the edges of open shafts. Shift bosses were usually Cornish because this was a job that demanded experience. His drillers, also Cornish, thought of themselves as only a step or two below the shift boss. Engineers and technicians came next in this hierarchy, then timber men, and finally the muckers and common laborers. Off the job and on the surface, for the most part, democracy reigned. Altercations between Cornish drillers and the Italian and Irish muckers sometimes flared, but lingering grudges were supposed to be left at the surface. In the dangerous underground world these men descended into, it was paramount that each individual should look out for the other.

Miners were said to develop a sixth sense that alerted them to danger. Tunnels were kept clean of trash and debris to prevent smells that were alien to that of the rock. Miners were always on the alert for any faint odor that might indicate poisonous gas or perhaps smoke. A flickering candle might mean oxygen deprivation or nothing more than a simple draft. Tunnels, even those through solid granite, tended to shift, buckle and collapse due to the incalculable internal pressures of the mountain itself. Men did not whistle or sing and talked only when necessary. They listened to the groaning and creaking of the shoring timbers hoping to interpret sounds that might indicate an impending cave-in. Rats infested some mines, and miners left them alone. There was a saying: "When the rats move out, so does the miner." Muckers watched the little Spanish mules that pulled the ore cars. If for any reason an animal began to leave an area on its own, the men usually followed, trusting the beast's ability to detect approaching disaster. They had their superstitions as well. Accidents were believed to happen in threes. It was considered bad luck to allow a woman into a mine. If a miner's clothes fell off the clothing hook in the changing house, it could well indicate the owner himself might suffer the same fate in the mine. If a candle fell from a tunnel wall or went out three times, it might indicate a disaster on the surface. Perhaps more colorful was the belief brought by the Cornish about ghosts called Tommyknockers. Thought to be the spirits of dead miners, they were known more for the sounds they made than any actual presence. Drillers claimed they heard them tapping from inside the walls, and some believed that, under certain circumstances, if they would follow those ghostly taps, they would be led to a richer body of ore. To encourage this, some men left small portions of their lunch behind. Invariably these offerings would be gone by the next shift, and while some argued that they had been eaten by the rats, others were not so sure. A vengeful Tommyknocker might steal a man's lunch bucket, blow out a candle, hide tools, kick the rungs out of a ladder, or even cause minor cave-ins. Those not inclined to believe in these ghostly sprites usually kept their doubts to themselves because there were frequent happenings for which there were no logical explanations. But beyond any possible influence from a spirit world, there were the very real possibilities of sickness, accidents and death.

In addition to having lungs filled with rock dust, men who lived in the cramped mine boarding houses ran the risk of contracting consumption (tuberculosis). Working in damp conditions and coming out into dry, sub-zero mountain air exacerbated the condition. Even for healthy lungs the shock of going from mine to mountainside often proved dangerous. Pneumonia probably killed as many men as accidents. Falls were usually the most frequent cause of injury in a mine. In addition, muckers often had

An Ophir logging camp. Courtesy Montrose County Historical Museum. Photo by Ben Walker.

hands or feet crushed by the ore cars which averaged one ton each when full. When electricity was introduced into the San Juans, bare wires carrying 800 to 900 volts ran along the walls and down the shafts waiting for any unwary hand or body that might brush against them. Occasionally at the higher mines, lightning would strike the ore car tracks leading into a mine and would follow them all the way to a working crew with fatal results. Machine operators suffered too. Pumps and engines were seldom protected by safety shields, and men would be caught by their clothing and pulled into spinning wheels. Steam burns were common, and on occasion a boiler would blow up and fatally scald any and all who might be working close by. Air compressors ran extremely hot and if an unwary operator added the wrong oil, it could vaporize and blow the machine to bits. The San Juan region led the nation in its use of mechanized equipment. New technology often had to be experimented with by men who had little or no prior training. Such experimentation carried risk. Many San Juan mines were at or even above timberline, and altitude sickness was common. The standard medication was several stiff drinks after the shift was over. Working at elevations of more than 12,000 feet above sea level, more than one man's heart gave out swinging an eight pound hammer at fifty blows per minute. Fires too caused deaths. On November 20, 1901, an underground fire in the Smuggler-Union Mine near Telluride suffocated twenty-four miners.

Whatever the hazards, mining was an end in itself for most of the Cornish professionals, engineers, and machine operators. For muckers and other laborers it was often a step upwards towards something better. In those early days most men in the San Juan region could say that they had done their time in one mine or another. From there they opened stores or businesses, farmed or ranched, or found a steady position with the railroad. Most never forgot the time they had spent underground, and however they felt about it, the experience helped create a bond of understanding pervasive throughout the San Juan region for decades afterwards.

CHAPTER SIX –
Wives and Sweethearts

Roughly twenty-five percent of the San Juan miners were married men who had brought their wives and children with them. Others were separated from families who were still back East or even in Europe, and a smaller percentage had sweethearts and fiancées they corresponded with. In the case of the latter, it was not uncommon for a man to take the summer off and return home to marry and then bring his new bride west before winter. There were also a limited number of weddings in the mining towns and camps. From 1874 through 1881, Silverton recorded twenty-three. Perhaps because of the rarity of local weddings, they were often elaborate and well planned. Grooms ordered wedding rings from back East; Tiffany & Company in New York was a favorite. An average ring would easily dispense with two weeks' worth of wages for the purchaser. Brides dressed in elaborate gowns, and a community celebration was almost always in order.

Regardless of whether a girl was married in the East or locally, one thing she could count on was a "shivaree" A few days after the couple had settled in and presumably was in bed, neighbors and friends gathered outside the dwelling and began a terrible clatter by banging on pots and pans. The groom and his recent bride were expected to greet and treat everyone present. The ladies were given candy while the men preferred cigars. In some instances the groom was expected to buy his fellows a drink in one of the area saloons at a later date. If a couple attempted to ignore the efforts of a shivaree crowd, they faced the threat of revelers climbing onto the roof and stuffing rags down the chimney. No right-thinking woman wanted her home smoked up, so surrender was usually immediate. Shivarees, while noisy and a bit wild, were a way to welcome the new couple into the married community, and no one meant any real harm.

The high mountains of southwestern Colorado had their own methods of greeting a newly arrived woman from the East. In a day when pale complexions were the style, brides were horrified by what high altitude, sun, and dry air did to their skin. Sunburn and freckles appeared almost immediately. The dry air left their lips cracked and bleeding. One remedy

A miner and his bride.
Author's Collection.

suggested by the miners was to rub ear wax on the affected part. New residents were told that mountain air was filled with antiseptic ozone, was healthy for the heart, and stimulated the brain. True or not, there were plenty of other things to stimulate a young bride's brain beyond the rarefied air.

Her first challenge was to make a home for herself and her new husband. In the days before trains that was a challenge. Her parents and family helped by sending her belongings west but seldom in a single shipment. Loss and breakage were frequent, and wagon freight could prove interminably slow. So it was that a bride often began housekeeping with empty packing boxes for furniture. To lend a touch of civility, she covered them with calico cloth. With no cupboards or closets the next best thing was to pound nails into the walls to use as hangers. Pack rats and mice were not deterred by nails, so a prudent homemaker acquired one or two empty cigar or chewing

Moving day for a miner,s family. Courtesy Montrose County Historical Museum.

tobacco shipping cases. The insides of these heavy wooden boxes were lined with zinc-covered iron and they made good storage trunks for fancy clothing and other precious items. Beds were nearly always homemade and, prior to the 1890s, lacked both springs and mattresses. A large sack of mattress ticking was filled with straw or grass and placed on top of ropes woven across the bed frame in both directions. Straw mattresses attracted bedbugs and other crawling creatures, and the ropes tended to stretch, leaving the occupants sleeping in what more resembled a hammock than a bed. This was to be expected, and the old saying, dating back to at least colonial times, could be taken literally: "Sleep tight and don't let the bed bugs bite." Periodically a husband was expected to tighten the bed ropes, and his wife would place the mattress sack outside in the dead of winter in hopes that the freezing temperatures would kill whatever vermin might have taken up residence inside. This helped, but bedbugs, in particular, often proved hardier than the people they slept with.

House floors could become extremely cold, so an industrious woman saved all her rags and ripped them into strips which she then braided into small rugs that could be placed at strategic locations around the house. In

Miners, families and a board and batten house. Courtesy Ouray County Historical Society.

some cases she spread straw or grass on a floor and nailed canvas or carpet down over the top.

Then there were the necessary outside chores, not least of which included keeping a path shoveled to the outhouse during winter. A woman fought snow burn and more freckles and her chapped and cracked lips continued to prove bothersome, but through it all she kept her courage. Hanging from at least one of the walls of her home would be a plaque or two containing an inspirational saying. "A merry heart maketh a cheerful countenance," was a local favorite. Cheery countenances became more common as conditions improved for these early pioneering women of the San Juan silver camps. The 1870s were the most difficult years because everything had to be freighted in by wagons an expensive undertaking and one which often left furniture scratched, marred, and frequently in pieces. By the early 1880s, when the railroads arrived, that changed. Shipping rates dropped drastically, and freight usually arrived in pristine condition. It was now possible to bring in the heavy, dark walnut furniture so favored at the time. Bricks and building materials were also hauled in, and exquisite homes began to appear in the bigger San Juan towns. The proud new owners could take the train to

Denver for shopping trips that extended into a week or more of staying in fine hotels, dining out, and shopping. The lady of the house brought back furniture, carpets, fancy window shades, exotic birds, and even goldfish. Proper Victorian homes of the period were crammed – every nook and corner with decorations of one kind or another. The residences of many of the newly rich also boasted servants as well as nannies hired to care for the children.

For most San Juan homemakers, less ostentatious surroundings were the rule. In addition to cooking, cleaning, tending children, sewing, and tending the stoves in winter, there were also clothes to wash. Many women made their own soap by saving used lard and cooking fat, then boiling it with lye (some even made their own lye) in large backyard kettles. On wash day white items were boiled vigorously over an outdoor fire and stirred with a hand carved paddle known appropriately as a "battling stick." These devices were also pressed into service as a disciplinary tool against the backside of an offending male child. Girls were seldom spanked. A stern look or a few sharp words usually sufficed. Colored clothing was scrubbed by hand in cooler water to avoid fading out the dye. Most women and their participating daughters had no love for wash day especially in winter.

A majority of homemakers shopped from catalogs after 1880, and could purchase about anything they had the desire and money for. Sewing machines cost from twelve to fifteen dollars. A large claw–foot oak table ranged from four to ten dollars with matching chairs costing a few cents over a dollar each. A complete bedroom set could be had for ten to twenty dollars, and bedspreads ranged between one and two dollars. A six by nine foot carpet cost an average of two dollars. A fifty-six piece porcelain dinner set averaged four dollars. For baby, a twenty piece outfit, including two rubber diaper pants, cost six to nine dollars depending on how much lace was desired. Women also ordered material to make clothing, curtains, and even bedding. Sheets and pillow cases could be made at home for half the cost of factory-finished items. The average miner took home three dollars a day throughout the latter third of the nineteenth century, and prices for consumer goods remained fairly constant. In many cases they actually decreased.

Like her eastern sisters, a San Juan woman spent a good deal of her time cooking, but she faced a unique set of problems. High altitude meant that it took longer for her to prepare a meal. Water boiled at a lower temperature than down in the flat country making that mode of cooking more time consuming, and in the case of items like dried beans, almost impossible. Consequently most cooks preferred to fry food. This process required lard, lots of lard, which came in fifty pound cans. It was considered not only necessary for cooking and baking but was thought to be essential for a person's health. Hard working men liked biscuit and pie dough to contain as much of this rendered pig's fat as possible, with just enough flour to hold things together. High altitude also made baking bread more difficult for the uninitiated.

Gardens were essential for homemakers in the nineteenth century, but again the high altitudes and short summers of the Colorado mountains limited the possibilities. Many women did manage to harvest radishes, table onions, lettuce, beets, and carrots as high as 9,000 feet elevation. They experimented with flowers, and those that grew were carefully nurtured with left-over wash water.

For San Juan homemakers, most of the food used was purchased locally. Edibles could be acquired at a variety of locations. Most towns had at least one bakery, butchers had separate shops, and while some stores did specialize in food stuffs, most variety stores and even hardware stores stocked a selection of edible items. Grocery stores also carried household items normally available in hardware stores. Competition helped keep prices in line.

As far as variety, a homemaker was limited. She could purchase dried beans, peas, and rice. There was flour, macaroni, cereals, oatmeal, crackers, vinegar, molasses, raisins on the stem, and brown sugar that came in large wooden barrels. A great treat for neighborhood kids was to be allowed to scrape out whatever sugar remained after the barrel was empty. Pickles came in wooden barrels as well. Canned fruit, vegetables, and syrup were sold in five pound containers. Dried peaches and apricots were on hand year around. In season the trains brought in apples and other fruit as well as a variety of vegetables. Many families took advantage of cabbage and made sauerkraut in the fall and stored it through the winter. To get a hand up on the competition, some grocery stores sent a wagon around in the morning to take grocery orders that would then be delivered to a housewife's door after lunch.

If a women wanted meat she went to the butcher, and, if prudent, she went early to get the best cuts. Beef, the perennial favorite, was butchered behind the shop and then halved or quartered and displayed in the front of the store for the purchaser to inspect and to select the cuts desired – nearly always steaks or boiling beef. Wild game was available periodically, and bear meat was popular especially for roasts. During cold weather it often proved more provident to purchase an entire quarter of beef, hang it in a secure shed behind the house, and cut off a piece of frozen meat with a saw whenever it was needed. Cold weather also froze eggs, which were kept in that state until they were ready to use. A majority of town families kept a few chickens and often a milk cow. Potatoes could not be allowed to freeze, so they were kept in pits beneath the house, and, in some cases, inside mine tunnels.

Despite the limits imposed, a mining camp wife prided herself in regards to the meals she prepared. A necessary accessory she often relied on was her cookbook. The more popular ones stretched to as many as six hundred pages and contained a variety of recipes that could be made with the limited ingredients available. Most cookbooks also included housekeeping hints and sections on human and veterinary medicine.

Food was never wasted. Leftover meat was chopped up, mixed with potatoes and onions, and fried up as hash the following day. Desserts were always popular, and families looked forward to puddings, cobblers, or mince pies spiked with a taste of brandy. The family dog survived on whatever scraps were left. On occasion a housewife found a tramp at her door begging for a meal. She considered it a part of her Christian duty to feed these vagrants.

Supper was the main meal of the day. If her husband worked the day shift in the mines, the family ate when he arrived home shortly after seven. If he worked the night shift, the family ate early enough to get father to the mine by seven. With stomachs full, it was time for spiritual food – prayers and a reading from the family Bible. Then with the children tucked into bed, the hard-working homemaker had time to sew and give thought to tomorrow's menu.

San Juan women were usually young. Few were over thirty-five and despite the sometimes rough and tumble frontier appearance of a mining camp, they seldom allowed their environment to affect the way they dressed. Underclothing consisted of an embroidered cotton chemise, linen or cotton drawers (the hems of which were nearly always decorated with embroidery or edged with lace), and a corset tightly drawn in from just above the waist to below the bust. A knee length petticoat or pantalettes went over white stockings or hose, and women wore the smallest shoes possible. Small feet were considered very attractive. Unfortunately for the stylish dresser, mountain winters demanded a few additional items. Extra petticoats were needed to protect a woman's legs, and in very cold weather, there was the option of wearing heavy, union-suit underwear. Nursing mothers wore special winter 'nursing vests' that partially solved their particular problem, although frost bitten nipples were a danger if they chose to travel by horse during extremely cold weather. In sleighs and wagons a woman could tuck herself beneath heavy lap robes. Winter coats were long and heavy, gloves were usually fleece lined, and a favorite winter hat of the time was made from glossy seal fur. The items of winter apparel that women universally hated were rubber covered overshoes or "arctics" as they were locally called. Heavy, chunky, and lined with thick felt inserts, they made the wearer's feet appear enormous.

Public buildings were often on the chilly side, so women wore winter dresses made from heavy material. Victoria Day, wife of famed Ouray newspaper editor David Day, owned a forty-pound dress made of black English satin. It was warm and stylish – both essential prerequisites for a San Juan lady. Pressure to dress properly came from males as well. Men expected a woman to be fashionably attired anytime she appeared in public, no matter who she was.

Although items like hats, gloves, coats, and shoes were purchased, many a woman preferred to make, or have made, at least part of her dresses and undergarments. In the case of the latter, a wealthy woman might own as many as six sets of underwear. In any case, a good seamstress was always in demand. The latest styles could be copied from magazines like *Ladies Repository* or *Godeys Ladies Magazine*, the latter of which also offered a mail order section for necessities such as perfume and items "peculiar" to female needs. In a time when bathing, even for women, was not an everyday occurrence, perfume was relied on heavily. Ladies even mixed it with castor oil or lard and worked it into their hair. It was said at the time that only if a woman's perfume overpowered the smell of a nearby horse, was she wearing too much.

That might have been the idea because horses were very much a part of these women's, lives especially during the warmer months. Many towns and camps boasted riding clubs with female membership only. Of course it was obligatory for participants to ride sidesaddle. With both legs primly positioned on one side of the animal, social decorum was preserved and style could be maintained as well. Specially made velvet riding skirts were so long that they had to be lifted and carried to avoid dragging the ground while the wearer was on foot. Once mounted, the skirts came to the belly of the horse, thus covering not only the legs but the feet of the wearer. It was also common to sew buckshot into the hem to provide weight and avoid any possibility that an errant gust of wind or a bounce might lift the skirt while the rider was in the saddle.

Women also frequented the local hot springs. Here a woman wore a short sleeved union suit that came to her knees, but the outfit was over-layered with a skirt and blouse – still quite revealing for the time. But at home style gave way to practicality. Even wealthy women reverted to simple calico dresses, and San Juaners might well have been in the vanguard of change, because their working skirts often came midway below the knees rather than reaching nearly to the ground. To preserve modesty, pantaloons were worn underneath and tucked into high button shoes. The same outfit could be worn on hikes and other summer outings. For backyard wash day activities a homemaker might even resort to wearing a pair of her husband's trousers beneath her skirt. However should she decide to make a quick trip into town, she would slip into a long dress. Winter and rough terrain might have influenced the way she dressed, but that influence remained bound to the styles and customs of the time.

What were fine clothes for, if they could not be flaunted a bit? Photography, available even before the Civil War, had previously been limited to special occasions and formal portraits because of cost. By the late 1870s prices had been reduced, and professional photographers were readily available. Interestingly enough, nearly one out of four Colorado photographers were women, and when trains arrived in the San Juans, female photographers made periodic trips away from their studios along the front range to spend a few days in the various mining towns. It could be a lucrative business. Photographs were commonly four inches by five and a half inches, but seven by nine inch prints were popular as well and sold for twenty cents each. Children found themselves in front of a camera perhaps more than they would have liked. The process could prove tedious, because slow exposure time meant that the subject had to remain absolutely still for up to thirty seconds. Photographers had a special stand with a forked yoke to place behind a child, invisible from the front, but fitting viselike on the back of the head to impede movement. Oval picture frames were used because many cameras of the time tended to cause the corners of a photograph to appear out of focus. Nearly everyone had their picture taken at least three times in their lives at their christening, wedding, and hopefully at their twenty-fifth wedding anniversary. Photographs were also taken of the dead, especially children, and many times this would be the only picture a family might have. Women, it would appear, had their pictures taken frequently. In 1885 when the Denver police began using mug shots of criminals, they did not, for several years, need to photograph a single woman prisoner (almost always prostitutes) because each one carried or had available, a recent formal photograph. Even these "fallen" ones had their pride.

San Juan women attempted to keep their lives in tune with their Victorian sisters from other parts of the country, primarily through reading. Books on social etiquette were extremely popular. It was of vital importance for a women to know exactly when, that she might wear her gloves during a formal dinner. During a ball she needed to be adept at sending and understanding as many as twenty different signals all dispersed by discreet movements of a hand fan. It proved a grand system to communicate to her sisters over the heads of unsuspecting men, although the attentive male could find these signals to his own benefit as well. Books could be purchased regarding marital relations, pregnancy and related medical problems, childbirth, birth control, and "marital duties" and responsibilities. Magazines for women were popular, and entire novels were serialized to come out weekly or monthly. Books and magazines were shared between friends, topics of interest were discussed, and new ideas disseminated.

Few women made the choice to come west willingly. That had been their husband's decision. They left behind family, comfort, and familiar customs, but few stopped to wallow in self-pity. Instead they formed support groups and developed their own social systems. In the early years there was little social distinction among 'proper' women. The further they lived away from the towns, the less social differences were in evidence. For women whose husbands struck it rich, their origins often kept them in close touch with their less wealthy neighbors. In many cases, American born wives mixed with immigrant women from Europe, overcoming language barriers through the commonalties of daily experiences. The one line that was firmly drawn was between "proper" women and those who made their livings in the bordellos and dance halls. The two sides never mixed.

Mining camp life had its advantages. In addition to a lack of social stratification, women also had a sense of freedom that would not have been openly tolerated either back East or in Europe. Respectable women were allowed to work and earn money, and, on occasion, became wealthy through their own ambitions. Businesses in the mining camps willingly allowed credit accounts in a woman's name. This practice extended even to Ute Indian women in the area who shopped on credit and faithfully paid their bills each month with proceeds gained from the livestock they raised and sold. Advertisements appeared regularly in local newspapers requesting female help in boarding houses, restaurants, and various retail establishments. The former two places were proper, because they were traditionally a woman's domain; the latter because most men could make more money mining or in construction. Jobs often went begging in the early boom years, and this gave local women additional leverage. Some worked for newspapers. At one point, a Durango paper even boasted a female editor. School teachers were in great demand with two out of three positions filled by women. Victorian male dominance did show however. Among the questions a school board could be expected to ask a potential teacher was what church she attended and could she play the piano (for worship services). She was paid ten dollars a month less than her male counterparts and was known in the classroom as Miss or Mrs., whereas a man was referred to as "Professor." Still it was usually a step up from conditions elsewhere.

To abuse a woman was the quickest way for a man to gain the disdain of his fellows, but this did not necessarily protect women. Early Colorado was a man's world. The 1890 census showed 100 females in the state for every 147 males. In the San Juans men outnumbered women in excess of three to one. Many males who came west during those years tended to be less committed to domestic life. More than one woman suffered the fate of being abandoned. In such a case she often had no way to make a living and support a family, so she quickly remarried and not always happily. Women frequently suffered beneath the domination of alcoholic husbands. During an 1880 funeral in Silverton, the minister was extolling the virtues of a deceased miner when finally, unable to take it any longer, the widow (known by all to have spent years of silently suffering the abuse of her alcoholic spouse) stood up and loudly asked the parson if he really knew who was lying in the coffin.

Marriage, for the gentle sex, came as early as fourteen. Few women in the San Juans were still single after the age of sixteen, unless they had just recently entered the region. The men they married were, on average, ten to twelve years older. It was not uncommon to find as much as a twenty year difference between the ages of a couple. Men had established interests in careers, the lodges they belonged to, local politics, and the community in general. Most were not cruel, rather just men of their time, and the desires and needs of women did not normally count a great deal in their approach to life. Consequently their wives turned to other women, religious beliefs, and their children for support and comfort. But bringing a child into the world was often a woman's worst fear. Complications and even death were routine.

A cabin in the trees. Courtesy Ouray County Historical Society.

Pioneering life was nearly always more difficult for a woman than a man, and the San Juans were no exception. Living conditions, at least during the 1870s, were more primitive than a woman would have encountered back

East or in Europe. In addition the high altitude, combined with a less than perfect diet, tended to complicate pregnancies. Less oxygen made a pregnant woman want to sleep more, and a lack of vital nutrients sapped her strength. Still she had a home to maintain. San Juan doctors frequently encountered this condition and called it pretty much what it was. Women "overdid" themselves. The prescribed treatment was to hire someone who could help with cooking and other household chores. In some cases neighbors lent a hand. In other instances temporary help would be hired, often a local girl old enough to cook, clean, and help handle other domestic chores.

In many instances pregnant women preferred not to rely on a doctor at all. This was an age when proper Victorian ladies hid their freshly laundered undergarments between bed sheets on the clothes line to dry. Although it was considered necessary for a male shoe clerk to touch their feet, even this experience was considered distasteful. An examination by a doctor ran completely counter to everything a woman had been taught. First of all, most physicians still placed their ear directly on a patient's chest to listen to the heart. If an obstetric exam was conducted, the doctor first lubricated his hand with either soapy water or unsalted lard an experience few women were willing to submit to.

A particular incident shows the lengths one young woman went to, to avoid a doctor's touch. When she discovered herself pregnant for the first time, she used her husband for a go-between with a physician in Telluride to monitor the pregnancy right up to birth. Both she and her husband were college graduates.

If available a women preferred the services of a mid-wife and for good reason. She stood a far greater chance of death from complications of "puerperal fever" when a physician handled the delivery than when under the care of a female mid-wife. The problem came primarily from doctors refusing to wash their hands. In a study done in Europe in 1842, it was shown that the death rate for delivering mothers was one hundred and twenty per thousand births when attended to by physicians who did not practice rudimentary sanitation standards. If a doctor washed his hands with soap and water before attending the birth, the death rate plummeted to twelve deaths per one thousand births. Nevertheless, doctors proved stubborn, particularly in the American West.

An obvious solution was to train women doctors, and these were available, in small numbers, in Colorado by the early 1870s. Unfortunately, the Colorado Medical Society voted two to one to exclude them from even attending medical society meetings in the state. In 1896 the women doctors in Colorado formed their own state medical society. Most female physicians established their practices along the front range, and once train travel was established, a respectable number of San Juan women, at least those who could afford to, chose to go to Pueblo for childbirth. For most mothers-to-be this was not an option, and they delivered at home under the care of a midwife. These women with their experience, female intuition, and common sense were the best that was available locally. As the years passed, women doctors did attempt to establish practices in the San Juans. In 1887 a female physician opened a practice in Durango, the largest town on the Western Slope at the time, but she left eleven months later after having been unable to build a viable practice. The local newspapers barely mentioned her existence and never listed her full name, although they gave considerable free publicity and a big welcome to any male physician who set up a local practice. Another woman tried Durango in 1894 and managed to stay almost three years. Telluride had at least three female doctors come and go between the years of 1889 and 1897. Meanwhile women continued to suffer from vaginal tears, prolapsed uteruses, painful pudendal hernias and anemia. The latter condition, recognizable by a competent physician, could easily be treated, but again, many women suffered and even died rather than seek professional medical care.

In one sense, San Juan women were not completely cast adrift. Many owned either a copy of *Marriage Guide, Or Natural History Of Generation* or *The Married Woman's Private Medical Companion*. Both of these volumes went through numerous editions and were surprisingly up to date. Methods of birth control were covered, but the most common technique, and one that obviously did not work too well, was for a mother to nurse a child as long as possible in hopes of delaying the next pregnancy. In 1873 Congress passed the Comstock Law which forbade further advertising for any birth control device or information and allowed postal authorities to confiscate any that might pass through the mail. One reason for the law was the desire to help reduce abortions, particularly among prostitutes. In desperation, some women would turn to advertisements for such things as "Madam

Dean's French Female Pills" in the hope of inducing a chemical abortion. Sometimes these dangerous concoctions worked, but often they did not. Various individuals (usually female) would also perform abortions but the death rate was as high as forty-five percent and survivors were nearly always left sterile. With no other real choices, most San Juan women chose to yield to what was inevitable, having babies. Jessie Fremont Pollock lived in Silverton and gave birth to thirteen children, eleven in a two-room cabin. She died at age forty-two of a stroke. Margaret E. Donovan, Missouri born and of Irish stock, married a Silverton butcher, bore eleven children, lost three of them, collapsed, and died at nearly the same age as Jessie her health sapped from years of hard work and child bearing.

Whatever hardships they bore, San Juan women could be expected to rally towards brighter times. They, like their husbands, usually portrayed an attitude of optimism that became especially evident in their recreational and social activities. Winters were often necessarily a time of enforced social isolation because of harsh weather, but by February, the days were growing noticeably longer and spring was not far away. Valentine's Day was celebrated in the San Juans, particularly among the women, and they traded either handmade or commercial cards. Comic themes were popular and these were usually delivered or mailed anonymously. Young women of courting age could expect to be the recipients of cards as well, but these were more serious in nature. Cards were also sent and exchanged at Easter and Decoration Day. First observed on May 30, 1868, the latter holiday was to honor Civil War dead. Photographs taken in Telluride during the 1880s show veterans, both Union and Confederate many in uniform, marching side by side in Decoration Day parades. Afterwards the crowd gathered at the local cemetery; the debris of winter was cleaned away, and flowers placed on the graves. This was a poignant time for many mothers because of the number of babies and small children they had buried. Prior to 1900, nearly eighty percent of the burials in the Old City Cemetery north of Lake City were those of children under the age of five.

July and August were special times for outdoor activities in the Colorado mountains. By late June, wild strawberries were ripening and groups of women, along with their smaller children, hiked up the mountainsides in search of the succulent fruit. During the Fourth of July celebration, a three-day event, the ladies served up bowls of strawberries swimming in fresh cream, and sprinkled liberally with sugar. These were sold to the crowds of miners who attended the celebration, and the money was used for a variety of civic and church projects. Homemade ice cream was also churned and sold as a money making project. While the menfolk enjoyed mining contests and horse races, their wives set up displays and exhibits that included sewing, cooking, and canning. Fresh strawberry preserves were naturally a favorite.

When the strawberry season began to give out, wild raspberries were ripening, often in profuse quantities. Within a short time of a mining camp or town's establishment, the surrounding mountainsides were cut clear of trees. The newly bare slopes proved perfect for the rapid proliferation of raspberry thickets. Wild raspberry preserves slathered across a hot buttery biscuit in the dead of winter was said to have had no equal. But with work came fun as well. Empty dynamite boxes were secured, one on each side of a docile and dependable burro. Babies, small children and picnic lunches rode up the mountainsides in these conveyances, and ripe raspberries rode back down. Such outings were probably looked forward to as much for the social interaction and recreational value as they were for the practical aspect of berry picking.

On other occasions, with no pretense concerning work, women went for hikes, accompanied by all who chose to go along including elderly women. Summer horseback rides were also popular. These were often a mixed group activity for younger individuals, but women frequently went on their own rides. The Telluride Women's Riding Club generally had more than a dozen active members who owned their own horses and others who rented from local stables. The group began with custom-made sidesaddles upholstered with imported Belgian carpeting, but as they began to explore higher into the San Juans, they dispensed with Victorian propriety and began riding with the same equipment and in the same manner as the men. The fancy sidesaddles and long velvet riding habits were retained for more formal rides in the valley when the menfolk were along.

December was the primary month for social dances and formal balls. As Christmas approached, some towns had a dance nearly every night. Fort Lewis, an army post west of Durango, sponsored an annual full-dress military ball to which the socially connected elements of the town flocked as much for the food as the dancing. Post cooks saw to it that the guests lacked for nothing. There were cakes, salads, fresh fruit, preserves, newly churned butter, and hot biscuits. There were pickles and a wide selection of cold meats including hickory-smoked ham. There was a big bowl of white sugar cubes (a novelty at that time), served with silver tongs, and used to sweeten steaming cups of coffee or glasses of cold lemonade. Formal balls were covered by the local newspapers, and social mavens of the day could count on reading a detailed account of the ball and the gowns that were worn.

Community dances were usually held in less ostentatious surroundings, but the food could be counted on to be nearly as good. Children were welcome, but as the evening progressed, many would gravitate towards corners where piles of coats were lying in heaps. They would burrow in and sleep until extracted by their parents for the trip home. Dances of all kinds were considered prime courting time for the unattached. Drinking at these affairs, or coming to the dance already inebriated, was not tolerated because of the presence of the ladies.

Styles were elegant. Author's Collection.

It did not take a special holiday to bring about a celebration. When new mines opened, area residents, including the women, were often invited to share in the celebration. On July 29, 1878, an eclipse of the sun nearly closed down the San Juans as large crowds gathered on mountainsides, picnic baskets in hand, to witness the event.

Even the deep winter snows were turned to advantage by the more adventurous female spirits. A surprising number took up skiing on hand-carved boards up to eleven feet long and guided by a stout pole they would drag along on either side of them in the snow. On occasion the more daring would persuade the local mail carrier to be their instructor. These were men who routinely crossed the San Juans in the dead of winter with forty pound mail sacks on their backs, and routes of up to twenty-five miles a day often in blizzard conditions. Perhaps such men could better sympathize with students who attempted to descend a mountain, at high speed, encumbered by heavy, ground-length skirts.

Beginning in the 1880s, railroads brought other entertainment to the San Juan towns. Durango hosted its first circus in 1883. Local Ute Indians, hearing about elephants for the first time, came and camped beside the huge beasts, just so they could observe them. The sight of the animals' trunks was said to have reduced many of the normally serious warriors to howling fits of laughter. Theater companies, minstrels, and medicine shows also broke up the social monotony from time to time.

There was one social diversion that San Juan ladies used to their advantage. Quilting bees were a women-only affair, and while needles flew and new quilts took shape, so did a quest for greater equality. Two topics of discussion could be counted on at these gatherings, temperance and female suffrage. Women, better than the men, could see the far-reaching effects that drinking had in the mining camps. Temperance was a movement that would eventually, for a short time at least, see the banning of alcoholic beverages on a national level. The desire to vote also provided fire for many sewing bee discussions. This was not an issue that women were at liberty to discuss openly with their male counterparts. Men were under social constraints not to talk politics either to or in the presence of ladies, although Colorado women had been given the right to vote in local school elections in 1876. Unfortunately any proposal to allow increased voting rights for women would have to be made by the men. Publicly, male voters showed sympathy for the idea of female suffrage, but when faced by the issue at the ballet box, these same individuals tended to vote no. The voting records in the mountain counties of southwestern Colorado proved the men to be especially resolute concerning this issue. Eventually Colorado did give its female citizens the right to vote, and sexual equality took a long step forward in the mining towns and camps of the San Juans.

Much had changed in a generation. Tents and crude shacks were for most, little more than distant memories. The San Juan towns had become brick and stone. Trains, telephones, and electricity had brought tremendous changes and comforts. There were schools, churches, and social traditions firmly established. Through it all were woven the strands of civility and culture patterned by women who, in their own special ways, had been instrumental in carving out and helping to build a silver empire.

CHAPTER SEVEN –
Boom Town Kids

The early years in the San Juan mining camps were adventurous times, not just for the adults involved, but for their children as well. Everything was new and different. The crisp, sharp, mountain air contained a sense of restless urgency. Construction was everywhere, and changes occurred on a day-to-day basis. New mines opened, and fortunes were made and lost, sometimes in a matter of hours. Hundreds of horses, mules, and burros crowded the dusty streets, and new faces were constantly coming and going. It was in this environment that the miner's children lived and played.

Most were born in log cabins or two-room shacks, their mothers tended to by a mid-wife. Their first beds were clothes baskets, and proud mothers dressed them in gowns so long that when the baby was held, the hem nearly touched the ground. Many took their first horseback ride snuggled into a sling made from an old table cloth and attached to their father's back. They drank from their mother's breasts, and when only a few weeks old learned to swallow oatmeal, puddings, and other soft foods. The philosophy of the day demanded a plump baby, so they were fed often. When they could walk, their mothers made their first pair of footwear from the recycled tops of an old pair of her own high button shoes. When time came for the weekly bath, a galvanized tub was placed near the kitchen stove, warm water added, and baby was scrubbed first, followed by older sisters, then brothers, then mother, and finally father. Warm water was heated on the stove and added as needed.

Mothers carefully watched their babies for any signs of illness. In the last third of the nineteenth century, it was not unusual for forty-percent of the children to die before their fifth birthday, especially in the rough and tumble camps of the San Juans. During the warmer months, many babies suffered from almost incessant diarrhea. There were no window screens, and flies moved freely between backyard privies, animal manure in the streets, piles of garbage, and the objects a baby touched or the food it ate. Too many times, already weakened from diarrheal dehydration, a childhood disease like measles, chicken pox, or whooping cough was enough to nudge a small

Parents tried to get children photographed at least once. Author's Collection.

child into the cemetery. Doctors were expensive. A local town call cost three dollars, a day's wages for the average miner. If travel was involved, the bill might easily climb to ten dollars. Consequently, the mother tended to be self-reliant and doctored a sick child herself. She would call a physician only if all else failed, and sometimes, by then, even if professional medical care could help, it might come too late.

Some parents did not name a child until it was several weeks old, and it was usually through intense religious beliefs that a mother was able to accept the loss of not one but two, three, or more of her babies in the course of a lifetime. Little girls were buried in white dresses, and custom dictated that they be carried to their graves by young women also dressed in white. Small children themselves developed a stoic attitude after seeing so many of their playmates taken away. They were taught that they went from the sickbed directly into the arms of the angels and did not question otherwise. It was a favorite game for them to provide a funeral for pets and other dead

A boy's first trip to the photographer.
Author's Collection.

creatures they happened upon. Bugs and song birds were laid to rest beneath tiny tombstones made of mud.

Children began school at age five, although it wasn't unusual to find them in class a year earlier. They did their figures on small stone slates bound in wooden frames. Fancy ones folded over like a book. Their beginning curriculum centered on reading and writing. They practiced making letters over and over. Memorization was important. The smallest children began with practical adages like, "Little people should have long ears, but short tongues." As they grew older they moved on to poems and Bible verses, and demonstrated their knowledge in programs for their parents. Once basic reading and writing skills were firmly in hand, students moved on to mathematics. Multiplication tables were expected to be memorized up to 20 times 20. Geography was a favorite subject for all students. It was their primary window to the outside world. Singing was important, and students learned, by heart, many of the popular songs of the day.

San Juan schools were among the best in Colorado. Author's Collection.

The school year generally ran from September through part of May. It was the teacher's responsibility to come early enough to light a fire and warm the building. She generally had to carry a bucket of drinking water to school each day. Any left from the day before would have frozen solid during the night. After school she was required to pick up the room and sweep the floor. In addition to her regular duties, there were the harsh winters and social isolation of the high mining camps to contend with, as well as rotating her living quarters among the families of the students she taught. Most young, single, female teachers opted to leave the profession after a year or so and marry. Courting came with its own built in difficulties. Teachers were required to observe curfews, and school nights were generally off-limits altogether. Male teachers had fewer constraints and generally held second jobs clerking in a local business establishment during the weekends. With such short tenure it was difficult for a teacher to bond with her students. Kids tended to stick together, and sometimes they put a teacher they did not like under intense pressure. Many times the object of their disaffection was only two or three years older than some of her tormenters. Resignations in the middle of a term were not uncommon. But teachers generally had the backing of the parents, and discipline was enforced with a bundle of green willow sticks tied together. Applied to a boy's backside this device generally proved adequate to deter further errant behavior. A wayward young female would be asked to extend her hand, palm side up, and receive a whack or two that way.

Students brought their own lunches, usually contained inside an empty syrup can with a wire handle attached for easy carrying. In winter, older students brought a small container of left-over coffee from home. This was poured into a community pot and warmed on top of the stove prior to lunch. Kids either walked or rode burros. During very cold weather they draped folded burlap or canvas across the animals' backs. Once at school these quasi-saddles were unfolded and used as blankets to keep the creatures a little more comfortable as they waited patiently through the day for the trip home that afternoon. Burros generally cost nothing as packers would often abandon their sick or injured animals in town or near a camp, and kids would bring them home to nurse back to health for their own use. By 1900 many of the San Juan school districts were providing transportation for students with either multiple seat carriages or open wagons rigged to serve the same purpose.

Children at play. Courtesy Ouray County Historical Society.

Kids played outside year around. School games included tag, follow the leader, duck-on-the-rock, shinny and one-hole-cat. These were all simple games that involved little more than intense physical activity, imagination and lots of running and yelling. There was seldom any playground equipment. From the 1880s on, baseball became popular. To purchase equipment, schools held box suppers. Girls and their mothers decorated cardboard boxes and filled them with enough edibles for themselves and one male companion. Each box was then auctioned off to the highest bidder. The idea was that the potential purchasers were not supposed to know whose boxes they were bidding on, but more often than not pretense ruled.

Half to two-thirds of the students ended their formal education with the eighth grade, but for those who wished to continue on, most of the San Juan towns provided a high school. These were nearly always substantial structures with the latest text books and educational equipment. Local mine owners and engineers were proud of their schools and usually saw to it that there was an up-to-date science laboratory. San Juan students graduated with excellent basic educations and were able to successfully attend universities all over the country. Athletics played a role in the high schools too. The problem was that because of low enrollment, it was often difficult to recruit enough members for a team. In such instances the team rosters were completed from the ranks of former students or even young miners or freighters who lived and worked in the area and could arrange for time off to play.

Early childhood was generally a pleasurable time for the young. They played together regardless of social status, and unlike the majority of farm or ranch children of that time, their chores and responsibilities were minimal. They had time to roll hoops, walk around on homemade stilts, and play marbles and mumblety peg. In summer they hiked, fished, and explored the mountains rising above their homes. In winter they nailed old shoes to wooden barrel staves and had instant skis. They made their own sleds and toboggans. Telluride closed off one street each winter exclusively for kids to sled down. Other towns did the same. A dangerous game some participated in was to take a metal scoop shovel, hike up the mountain, and ride the shovel down across the hard snow at blinding speed. This was a trick they had learned from their fathers who often used the same technique to come down off the mountain after a day of work. Kids built elaborate snow forts, chose up sides, and had snowball wars. Sometimes the grownups would flood a level area and make them an ice-skating rink.

When they tired of games there were other things with which to amuse themselves. Ore haulers, often little more than teenagers themselves, frequently allowed kids to hitch a ride up the mountain in empty wagons, and mine workers had a casual attitude about kids exploring around a work area. Cuts, bruises, and even broken bones were sometimes the result. Occasionally boys would steal a box of a blasting caps and a few feet of fuse and sneak off to make their own firecrackers. Some lost fingers and eyes in the process. If an adult perceived what he or she considered as a truly dangerous situation, they would not hesitate to call a child down. Boys were always "Bub" and girls were addressed as "Sis" and obedience to a command from any adult was usually prompt. If not, word usually got back to the parents and that meant real trouble.

There were also rules of social etiquette that boys were expected to follow. With many Civil War veterans living and working in the San Juans, it was considered impolite to ask a man which side he had fought on. Nevertheless boys had a fascination about the stories they had overheard, and many collected, along with bones, rocks, and bird feathers, war memorabilia including old discarded pieces of uniforms which they would hide away to show to their friends. While doing so they might share a cigarette made of used coffee grounds, dried and wrapped in a piece of newspaper. They also collected and traded five-cent novels to read in private. These were neither lewd nor pornographic, but many parents disapproved and considered such writings as trash. In regards to sex, knowledge came from observing breeding livestock, and with dozens of prostitutes in every town, imaginations did not have to travel far. A few youngsters even boasted of having secret collections of postcards that portrayed poses of "shocking women" in skirts that extended half way down their thighs and wearing tight tops, although this was a hobby more for young, single miners. Another sport was to sneak out at night and spy on couples promenading the grounds outside a dance. On train trips boys and girls alike enjoyed spending time peering down through the open toilets and watching the track speed by. In Lake City boys could look forward to celebrating Washington's birthday by climbing a greased pole or attempting to capture a greased pig.

Male children in the mining camps were casual dressers and usually wore baggy, off-the-rack, store clothes or hand-me-downs from older siblings. In winter they put on one pair of trousers over the other and bundled up in bulky old Mackinaw coats discarded by their fathers or brothers. Their hair was allowed to grow all winter to be shorn off in the spring. If a dress-up occasion did occur, the style of the day was knee pants, long stockings and high-top shoes of soft leather that were notoriously easy to scuff.

Usually a boy did not lack for spending money in the San Juan towns. He could tend stock during the summers, split and stack firewood, or work part time in various stores. One of the better paying jobs was delivering newspapers. From the late 1890s on, the *Denver Post* offered the best wages, averaging from $1.00 to $1.25 per week. Most boys went no further than the eighth grade and some even less. The innocuous days of childhood were usually over at fourteen when a boy went to work full time in the mines, carrying tools or working in the breaker rooms, chipping away and separating worthless pieces of rock from the ore.

An early advertisement. Author's Collection.

Although little girls participated in many of the activities their brothers did, they were not allowed the same degree of freedom. Instead their lives were more closely aligned with those of their mothers. They wore ankle length dresses and played with rag or paper dolls for which they could order outfits out of a catalog. They used bits of glass or old assay cups they had salvaged at the mine dumps for dishes and held their own tea parties. By the age of five, a girl was expected to be able to successfully sew a small quilt. They also learned to crochet, and among their first projects was usually a 'pot husher.' These fit tightly around the rim of chamber pots and helped muffle the sound of the lid being replaced a sound that assaulted Victorian sensibilities. By age ten or eleven a girl was usually adept at running her mother's sewing machine and was beginning to make most of her own clothing. She was also able to cook and attend to normal household chores.

Much like her mother's, a little girl's social life was limited. There were school activities and she might take private piano or guitar lessons. Taffy pulls were popular during the colder months. She participated in evening activities with the family, which often included reading to each other. Popular works included the classics, Shakespeare's plays, and novels by Sir Walter Scott and Charles Dickens. Poetry was also included on the family reading list. On the lighter side were serial stories out of popular magazines. Many children, and especially the girls, developed substantial literary backgrounds. At about the age of ten she was allowed to participate in dances where, in the hands of her father's friends (never boys), she learned squares, waltzes, schotisches, mazurkas, and polkas. Two or three years later she stepped out of her ankle length dress for one that reached the floor. She was now considered a woman. Like her mother, she wore no makeup. By fourteen (unless she chose to finish high school or, in rare instances, went away to college) she was eligible to be seriously courted – and to begin hearing the stern admonition, "If you don't want peaches, don't shake the tree."

Perhaps too soon, most girls found themselves married to a man nearly twice their age. The tree was shaken, and the cycle, known so well by their mothers, began anew.

CHAPTER EIGHT –
Beer and Brothels

America, following the bloodletting of the Civil War, became a nation on the move. Thousands of young men spread across the western half of the country to build railroads and to create new mining empires. They represented veterans from both sides of the recent conflict, as well as immigrants fresh from Europe and even Asia. Most were single and restless, and many had a propensity towards drinking. What they found during the boom years of the West did not disappoint them. In 1860 America counted roughly seventy-five thousand drinking houses. By 1880 that number had doubled and most of the growth had taken place in the new mining, transportation, and supply towns of the West.

Saloons were usually the first substantial structures to be built in these rough and tumble boom towns. In addition to their intended use, they served as sleeping quarters, court rooms, community centers, bulletin boards, and even churches. Nowhere were they more in abundance than in the mining towns with their potential for sudden wealth. The silver camps of the San Juans were no exception. The town of Ouray began with a few hundred residents in 1875, and within a matter of months counted nine saloons. Its older neighbor across Red Mountain Pass, Silverton, counted forty drinking houses. Lake City, Telluride, and Durango boasted similar numbers. Most of the camps higher up in the San Juans supported their own saloons.

In economic terms mining camp liquor sales proved quite profitable and less risky than mining itself. A miner often put everything he had into a promising claim, only to come up broke when an ore vein pinched out or suddenly became too low in value to bother with. This was not the case with a saloon. If there were miners, there were customers, and the trick was to separate them from their money and keep them happy at the same time.

Start-up costs were high, but with markups on product that reached four hundred percent, a mining camp saloon often paid for itself with the revenues from the first month of operation. Owners cashed in on the fact that most of their customers were young, single, and really had few other

A beer And liquor pack train. Courtesy Montrose County Historical Museum.

places to spend their money. Consequently a successful saloon was one that could reach out and accommodate more needs than just drinking. Typical were Durango saloons with catchy names like the Hub, Keg, Golden Room, Horseshoe and, The Office. Many served as mail drops or pickup points for regular customers. Barbers sometimes set up chairs in a back corner. Reading material was provided, and music was popular as well. Many of the higher class saloons boasted player pianos that provided all the latest music automatically and without the need of a pianist. Furniture and furnishings were tasteful and up to date. Free food was provided – mostly salty, snack-type items that would encourage a man's thirst. Towels were distributed at strategic locations so a drinker could wipe beer foam out of his mustache. Frequently a saloon had a safe where patrons could store their valuables before embarking on a drinking spree. Many establishments decorated their walls with mining paraphernalia and stuffed animal heads. Most had a big framed copy of Cassily Adam's famed painting of "Custer's Last Stand," of which thousands were distributed by the Budweiser beer company. Paintings of voluptuous women in various stages of undress also adorned the walls. Saloons frequently placed translucent paper high enough on the windows facing the street to prevent women and children from accidentally looking in as they passed by. Older boys sometimes lingered outside the swinging doors in hopes of a quick glimpse of one of the "nakkid ladies' as patrons entered or departed. Huge diamond dust mirrors were framed by liquor shelves behind polished hardwood bars imported from back East or Europe. The mirrors were considered a necessity as they allowed both patrons at the bar and the barkeeps, or bardogs as they were more frequently called, to keep an eye on their backs. Permeating it all was a blend of odors from spilt beer, tobacco spit, stale powder or dynamite fumes from patrons' clothes, cigar or pipe smoke, and animal manure tracked in off the street.

Destruction of saloon property was not tolerated, and most bartenders kept a sawed off shotgun behind the bar, as well as a wooden mallet that could be used to subdue a wayward drinker. For most customers fear of fines and jail time were enough to discourage destructive behavior. One miner who fired several shots in a Red Mountain saloon in 1886 was fined fifty dollars and spent twenty days in jail – typical punishment for the time. Most saloon patrons, especially when they were dressed up, thought twice before engaging in a bar room brawl while wearing a suit that had cost a week's wages. On particularly busy nights or holidays, bouncers were employed to keep an eye out for potential troublemakers. To further reduce the chance of problems, most Colorado towns had laws forbidding the employment of women in the drinking houses. Still there were times when crowds would become boisterous, and brawls did result, including an occasional shooting, although knives were usually the weapons of choice in the San Juan camps, particularly among recent European immigrants. Silverton, with a population of 1,200 inhabitants in 1885, often attracted as many as 3,000 miners from surrounding towns and camps for its Fourth of July celebration. On such occasions beer, at ten cents a glass, was consumed by the wagon load. Most beers of the time ranged from three percent alcoholic content up to ten percent – commonly referred to as "triple X." Beer was the drink of choice in the camps, particularly after the early 1880s when it could be brought in by train, and most of the bigger mountain mining towns boasted at least one brewery.

For those who preferred hard liquor, saloons provided that as well. Imported and bottled alcoholic drinks were available, but they were expensive. Most patrons preferred domestic varieties that came in wooden kegs. A high percentage of western hard liquor was locally made and seldom bore a government revenue stamp, which meant higher profits for the saloon owners. Unfortunately it also lacked the color and taste of legitimate alcohol from eastern distillers. To compensate, the makers would add such things as tobacco, burned sugar, ammonia, creosote, and sulfuric acid. Bar tenders frequently diluted the mixture with water. Miners called these concoctions names like "coffin varnish" or "corpse retriever." Although it is doubtful the stuff could really raise the dead, it crossed the bar at two shots for a quarter.

Patrons of the free coinage saloon.
Courtesy Ouray County Historical Society and Mike and Jennifer Fedel.

One reason for so many bars in the San Juan towns was because of the region's ethnic diversity and this resulted in segregation among the alcohol crowd. Silverton, with its forty drinking houses, was typical. Swedes, Austrians, Italians and Cornish miners often had their own favorite saloons where language and cultural backgrounds were similar. Even Italians from northern and southern Italy preferred to drink and socialize with countrymen from their own region. Thrown into this assortment of ethnic groups were Confederate and Union veterans from the Civil War, who often went separate ways as well. All of these groups were broken down still further into miners, railroad men, freighters, and packers each occupation having a slightly different slant on life.

Separated from their families in England, Cornish miners mixed their nights of drinking with traditional songs and even church hymns. They were especially sentimental about Christmas. Homesick for little brothers, sisters and other relatives they had left behind, they, with others of similar mind, helped see to it that no local child was forgotten. Bags of candy, nuts, an orange, and sometimes a toy were distributed. During the Christmas holidays, sentimental music and even poetry often helped draw homesick saloon patrons of different ethnic origins closer together. It was not unusual for men, half way through an evening of drinking, to become emotional to the point of tears. Hard work, loneliness, and life in an unfamiliar place pushed some from social drinking to alcoholism and even insanity. Men who reached the point of delirium tremors were tied to their beds, and arrangements were made to have them committed to the insane asylum in Pueblo. Some miners simply drank themselves to death. Saloon keepers often paid for the funerals of alcoholics, and perhaps rightly so since they had often been among the best customers. Extreme drinking was considered disgraceful. When a young man died in Ouray in 1878, a grand jury was convened to determine the cause of death. It was common knowledge that he had drunk himself to death, but the jury discussed the fact that the alcoholic had a mother and sister back East who needed to be notified. After lengthy discussion, they concluded that death had been a direct result of heart failure. The coroner dutifully informed the family of that finding.

For those who preferred more than just sitting around drinking, playing cards, and swapping stories, there were the dance halls. While less numerous than drinking houses, these establishments were popular. For twenty-five cents a patron was entitled to one drink and one dance, although usually he was expected to spend an additional fifteen cents to purchase his partner a drink as well a shot glass of cold tea usually. Dance hall girls made their money based on a percentage of both dances and drinks she sold in an evening.

Relaxing in a miner's shack. Courtesy Ouray County Historical Society.

For a few cents more, a man might take in a stage show. Most mining towns had what passed for variety entertainment. Ouray was typical with the Gold Belt Theater. It held an impressively large crowd, sold drinks, and for those who wished had a side entrance leading to rooms where more sensuous pleasures could be indulged. The Gold Belt was never intended for families, but it did attract some of Ouray's leading male citizens.

"Leg dramas" were the most popular shows. Well endowed actresses sang, recited verse, acted out skits, and showed enough flesh to make both silver and gold coins fly onto the stage from the hands of approving audiences. A talented woman could do very well. Lillie Langtry shocked western audiences by removing her clothing down to her slip during each presentation of a particular play and was able to retire a few years later, reputedly the richest single woman in America.

Periodically one mining town or camp would challenge a neighbor by proposing a prize fight. An article in the *San Juan Democrat* that appeared

April 18, 1889, was typical. "We the sporting men of Mineral Point have an unknown that we will match to fight the winner in the Strong Boy Jones and George Cooper contest for $500...(and winner take gate receipts), London prize ring rules to govern." It isn't known if the offer was accepted, and like so many early San Juan towns, Mineral Point lasted only a few years before being abandoned. Fight purses frequently reached a thousand dollars, a substantial gain for a hard fisted miner who normally made three dollars a day with a third of that going for food and lodging.

In other instances entertainment sometimes took a different direction. Gang leader and bunco artist Soapy Smith owned a reclining figure of cement and plaster that had supposedly been dug up near Creede. This "petrified man" sported a short tail and cost twenty-five cents to view. Periodically Smith would gather an audience and deliver a lecture regarding the creature's evolutionary origins.

If two-bit entertainment was not enough for a man's appetite, there were always the gaming houses. The San Juans offered keno, roulette, faro, craps, chuck-a-luck, stud, and straight-draw poker. To stay sharp and alert, dealers worked four-hour shifts. Soapy Smith, when he wasn't lecturing about his petrified man or seeing to his other shady enterprises in Creede, frequented the faro tables and tended to lose regularly. Although women had not been tolerated in either saloons or gaming houses in the San Juans during the 1870s and 1880s, times were changing by the early 1890s. Creede, the last San Juan boom town, counted dealers such as Killarney Kate, Calamity Jane, and Poker Alice (whose trademark was a lit cigar clenched between her teeth).

There was another questionable pleasure that, even in those tumultuous days, was only whispered about – opium dens. Blair Street in Silverton counted several, as did Ouray and most other San Juan towns. Archeologists have verified several sites by digging through the decayed contents of outhouses that once stood behind suspected buildings. They found scores of broken and smashed opium pipes that had been discarded down the toilet holes long ago. Opium smoking was brought to the San Juans by Chinese miners, who would take a small lump of black, gummy opium and smear it around the inside of a pipe bowl. The pipe was then heated over an open lamp, and the fumes inhaled until the user drifted into a dream-filled sleep. The habit spread from the Chinese to miners, prostitutes, and even an occasional proper Victorian lady. Civil war veterans tried opium to relieve chronic pain from old wounds and injuries. Prostitutes were often the heaviest users. Looked down upon by even the drunks, dope addicts were considered the lowest of the low and tended to keep their habits secret as long as possible. In 1892 Durango formed a chapter of a national group known as the Keeley Institute which was dedicated to helping deal with drug and alcohol abuse.

While drinking and other vices did play a predominant role in the lives of early San Juaners, there were many who abstained. Engineer City, a camp of 400 inhabitants between Lake City and Ouray, printed the following proclamation in the *Lake City Silver World*, of July, 1882. "Engineer City... can boast more inhabitants than Mineral City, Animas Forks, or Capitol City yet we have no saloon and the boys openly declare that with the grub put up at the Davidson Hotel they can do very well without any."

A saloon cartoon. Author's Collection.

Yet there would be one last gasp of wild living when the silver mines at Creede opened in 1890. In a matter of months eight to ten thousand people streamed into what would be the last of the San Juan boom towns. Saloons, dance halls, and houses of ill repute sprouted by the dozens – all competing for their share of wealth from the new mines. Con-men and bunco artists stood ready to relieve the unwary of their gold and silver and sometimes their lives. But the emergence of Creede brought other things as well. Within a few months the new town boasted most of the comforts of eastern towns: a railroad, telephone service, and even electric lights that burned until dawn. As it was with earlier boom towns, Creede mixed dreams with sweat, as silver by the ton was wrenched free from the flanks of nearby mountains. Newspaper editor Cy Warman of the *Creede Chronicle* explained it this way:

> Here is a land where all are equal
> of high and lowly birth
> A land where men make millions
> dug from the dreary earth,
> Here the meek and mild eyed burros
> on mineral mountains feed.
> It's day all day in the day-time
> and there is no night in Creede.

There might not have been any night in Creede, but within the shadows of the San Juan mining towns another institution flourished, and that was the "line" or "row" as many residents referred to it. In Ouray it could be found on Second Street; in Silverton on Blair Street; Telluride had Pacific Street; and Lake City counted Bluff Street – known by more upstanding folks as "Hell's Acre." Durango was home to the 555 Clipper, the Silver Bell and the Garden of Babylon. Other towns had establishments like the Ethiopian Temple of Pleasure, the Temple of Music, the Morning Star, the Monte Carlo, the Gold Belt and the Bird Cage. They were run by women who went by names like Frenchy Lulu, Slanting Annie, and Queen Marie. It was in these houses that a man might experience, for a brief time, the intimate company of a woman, the illusion of love, and the satisfaction of primeval urges. In most San Juan camps the male population generally hovered around eighty percent. Most of these men were single, under the age of thirty-five, and connected to their distant families by sporadic letters – if even that. It was under these conditions that the 'brides of the multitude' plied their trade. Telluride, at its height, counted between five and six thousand single miners and was home to an average of 175 "girls." They also had other names – daughters of desire, fallen angels, swamp angels, female divines, and soiled doves. In Ouray the girls referred to themselves as "chippies." The definition might have sprung from the idea of being lively and chipper, or it might have come from reference to poker chips. Either way the name had a hint of irony. Prostitutes were seldom chipper, and their lives and emotions were casually tossed about on the playing tables of life.

Accounts can be found about prostitutes who made their mark and were able to hold their own ground, but the number is minuscule. The majority of harlots and hookers after the Civil War years until the turn of the century left a far different story. Feminine opportunity was limited. A western woman could be a wife and mother in a day when labor saving devices were almost non-existent and birthing deaths common, or she could remain single, work as a servant, a cook, or laundress, possibly operate a boarding house – or she might become a prostitute.

Actual reasons for entering the flesh trade vary, but some girls and women wished to avoid a life of perceived drudgery for one that offered the possibility of excitement, social glamor, or even rebellion. Others entered the trade following failed marriages. Archeological excavations of the contents of brothel privies have turned up a considerable number of discarded wedding rings. Daughters of prostitutes were often snared into the trade sometimes at an incredibly young age. The July 7, 1876, issue of the *Rocky Mountain News* relates a police raid on a Denver brothel that netted two such girls, one age thirteen and the other eleven. The editor was so outraged that he advocated the hanging of any and all who had been involved.

High-class madams made frequent procurement trips back East to large cities where they searched for pretty sixteen-year-old girls from the slums and immigrant quarters. Their favorite targets were orphans to whom they promised a better and easier life than could be expected in the teeming tenements. Freshly scrubbed and wearing new clothes, the recruits would be escorted back to the mining camps and installed in private rooms in "boarding houses" furnished with the finest furnishings. Meals were served in-house, and the girls were given basic instructions in etiquette and manners. Residents were required to remit from their earnings five to six dollars per week for room and board. This was in line with what most miners paid for their own weekly living expenses, although they lived in far more austere surroundings. A parlor house girl had a brass or iron enameled bed, a dresser, rocker, lamps and lace curtains. Two meals a day were served brunch and an early dinner. She dined on steak and chicken and sprinkled Worchestershire sauce on her roast beef. A girl was expected to purchase seven to eight evening dresses and two or three street costumes all in the latest styles. Generally the money or the credit for these expenditures was advanced by her benefactor, the madam, who added on substantial interest charges. The young initiate began her work in the evening with the arrival of the clientele, men who were nearly always moneyed. Often the guests would dine with the girls, entertainment was provided, and then the young woman would retire to her room with her partner; at that point, pretense at Victorian decorum was dropped. The girls were purchased property and were expected to conform to their caller's every whim, even those that were degrading. Her services came high, up to thirty dollars for an evening, far more than a working miner could afford. Consequently the financially well-heeled Victorian gentlemen who dropped their money in a parlor house

A risqué "girlie" picture of the 1890s.
Author's Collection.

demanded the utmost in discretion; many were married. Although most of the earnings remained with the house, a girl received enough to eventually build a small fortune, although most squandered it on expensive clothing, liquor, or drugs. Exclusive boarding houses were rare in the San Juans and could more commonly be found in bigger cities like Denver.

By age twenty it was time for parlor house girls to move on. They had lost the sense of innocence so prized by their wealthy paramours, their faces had become too familiar, and often they had become cynical and sharp tongued. Many had developed an excessive taste for alcohol. The next step down was a brothel. These were more common in the mining camps, operated along the same lines as a parlor house, but the rooms were shabbier and Victorian mannerisms less pronounced. Business was brisk, and an encounter could cost from five to ten dollars depending on the length of time involved. Brothels were the residences of most girls until about the age of twenty-five. By that time nearly ninety percent had suffered bouts with venereal disease and pregnancies. Although prostitutes in Europe practiced various methods of birth control, few of their American co-workers did, partly out of ignorance and primarily because their clients would not have been tolerant. By age twenty-five alcoholism had become common, and not a few women had developed a dependence on opiates, particularly morphine, although most attempted to keep drug habits secret. In some cases they did take time out to have their babies. A few were kept on the premises. Others were sent east to relatives or even distant boarding schools. One Silverton prostitute faithfully sent money to an eastern boarding school until her daughter was grown but was careful never to let the girl know who or where her benefactor was. For a majority of prostitutes abortion was the preferred solution, either by someone who had practical experience nearly always another woman or, in many cases, the procedure was chemically self-induced. In either instance the result was frequently sterility or death.

When a woman became too difficult for either the madam or the customers to deal with, she was packed into the street with her trunk of clothing and usually went straight into the waiting arms of a pimp. Her next step down was into the cribs. Here she would find a new clientele who would ignore her caustic ways and her alcohol-reddened face. Cribs were usually small, two-room buildings. The back room was for living while the one that faced the street was strictly for business. Furnishings were Spartan, and prices commonly ranged between one and two dollars per encounter, depending on her desirability. Crib prostitutes kept very little of their earnings as most went to the men who controlled them. When she was not busy, her pimp expected her to be either at the door or window attempting to entice new customers. Meanwhile he directed business to her from the saloons and gaming houses. During holidays and on paydays, twenty-five to fifty encounters per night were not uncommon. Crib girls generally worked twelve-hour shifts. Part of the row was always open when off-shift miners were in town. Many women kept oilcloths stretched across the foot of their beds so customers would not have to remove their boots. Wasted time, at least to her pimp, was wasted money. When conditions became intolerable, crib girls escaped deeper into a bottle or a drug habit. Some took the risk of escaping completely and traveled to another mining town, where they usually ended up back in another crib. Disease, time, and personal constitution determined how long a woman worked the cribs, but it was seldom more than ten years. Her last step down was to become a street walker, and it was there that the term "two bit whore" found literal meaning. Others with diseased bodies and burned out minds found work at the infamous "hog ranches" located outside military posts, where young, immigrant soldiers had few scruples with whom or on what they spent their thirteen dollars a month.

For many prostitutes life ended between the ages of twenty-five and thirty-five. Death was often self-induced by a narcotics overdose combined with alcohol or by drinking carbolic acid, a common disinfectant of the time. Usually a woman's sisters-in-trade would pay for her funeral and buy her headstone. These can be found today in San Juan mountain cemeteries. They are generally marked with only a first name and date of death.

Following behind Telluride with its population of 175 girls, Silverton counted a maximum of about 135, and Ouray came in with nearly 100. Other towns and camps varied depending on population and time period. In some instances brothel operators would take their girls camping during the summer, set up tents close to the mines, work that area for a while, and then move on to fresher scenery elsewhere. In the bigger towns madams regularly took a carriage filled with her prettiest girls on Sunday rides through the business districts – to advertise as well as give the girls a recreational outing. A bordello in Telluride resorted to a more permanent form of advertising when it had part of its roof shingled to suggest the head of an alluring woman. The scene was only visible to miners coming down off the mountain. In some instances when mining activity slowed during the coldest months, bordellos would operate with a reduced staff and allowed some of the girls to take vacations back East. The only day of the year that the houses closed down completely was Christmas Day. Despite her contacts with the men who sought her favors, life for a San Juan prostitute was confining. She was not allowed into the "good" side of town, and in most instances, could not enter many of the businesses particularly those frequented by the more gentle elements of San Juan society. A proper woman would not venture into the side of town where her opposites lived. In Lake City town matrons would not even utter the name of the street where such activities took place. Clothing store owners sometimes discreetly opened their establishments after hours for specially arranged shopping ventures by girls from the row, because decorous women would not have shared the same shop with someone so morally inferior. In one breath they would refer to them as "poor fallen women," and in the next could and did threaten to bring about the firing of ministers who suggested that a church be used for a prostitute's funeral. Such affairs were usually held in the same part of town where the deceased had spent her working life, although most men of the cloth, despite criticism from members of their congregation or parish, were on hand to lend dignity and a sense of closing. It was not uncommon for some of the town's leading male citizens to attend a popular prostitute's funeral. Little or nothing is recorded as to how their wives might have felt in these instances.

Ironically it was the inhabitants of the parlor houses, the brothels, and the cribs who provided the financial support for most of the San Juan towns. There were no property or sales taxes, so necessary municipal revenues came from the drinking houses, the madams, and the girls who worked for them. Whereas saloons paid for an annual license, every girl of the row was "fined" two to five dollars per month. Each madam worked out her own arrangement with the town fathers. Often times she would "donate" money to help defray the cost of such things as fire-fighting equipment. She also had her own expenses to see to, and these could be substantial. A first-class parlor house was expensive to build, furnish, and operate. She had to pay servants and a musician. It was common for the more substantial houses to take up collections from their members to provide such things as food baskets for local needy families or even cash for the widows of men killed in mining accidents; all this anonymously, of course. On other occasions prostitutes risked their lives to serve as nurses to men fallen ill during various epidemics and who had no family to fall back on.

Generally the law left the row alone, but even the lowly cribs were required to operate with discretion, and everyone from madams to pimps were expected to keep their charges orderly. The primary reason was that containment facilities for female prisoners were almost non-existent in the mining towns. Silverton built a substantial jail during its heyday and set aside a barred and bolted bedroom for one female prisoner just off the kitchen of the living quarters for the law officer and his family. A slot was made through one wall to serve meals to the incarcerated.

The average age of a San Juan prostitute was twenty-three, and while most were Caucasian, a substantial number were Hispanic, Native American, black, or Chinese. Silverton's Ethiopian Temple of Pleasure employed only black girls. In a few notable instances prostitutes did marry and went on to lead more traditional lives, but these were in the minority. A few were shrewd enough to save their money and launch their own businesses and quite successfully too. Others enjoyed the way of life itself and threw themselves completely into their work. They too were in the minority. The majority of women who entered the flesh trade could expect an average of twenty years of steadily declining conditions. Their lives were wrapped in the bonds of social condemnation and the hypocrisy of a time when standards meant one thing for men and something entirely different for women. They looked for love and acceptance and found degradation and rejection. Despair was the companion of many, and their greatest comfort too often came from a bottle or an opiate. In the end most were left beneath forgotten stones or simple markers in the cemeteries of the towns they had worked in. Even here, their graves were separated and segregated from the general population.

CHAPTER NINE –
Bullets and Bandits

San Juan mining towns were unique among towns in the West. The region contained incredible quantities of high grade silver ore, but it was complex and demanded the very latest technology both for extraction and processing. This required substantial numbers of technicians, engineers, and experienced mine managers – many of whom had previously worked in Central and South America and the Great Lakes region. They were individuals who came with an ambition to make a profit and a lack of tolerance for uncivil behavior. They were allied with local businessmen, doctors, and other professionals, and together they saw to it that the miners, smelter workers, local cowboys, lumberjacks, freighters, and general laborers were kept in line.

Professional and business interests also controlled local politics. Ouray, for example, had a population of more than 2,500 people in 1877, one year after its founding, but it counted only 400 registered voters, the majority of whom came from the local elite. The town fathers knew what they wanted in terms of law enforcement and hired or elected the men they felt would best be able to enforce both the laws and the peace.

Cyrus W. Shores (referred to by most as Doc Shores) was elected sheriff of Gunnison County in 1884 and held the position for a number of years. He was a tall, hard muscled, ex mule-skinner with the inborn instincts of an investigator. This often proved an important skill for area lawmen, because high grade silver ore was a tempting target for clever thieves. Sometimes Shores would spend weeks following leads and rumors before making an arrest. He was a fair man with a flair for diplomacy and was respected even by many of those whom he arrested. Three men he had helped send to prison in Canyon City served their terms, came back to Gunnison, and told Shores that he had treated them fairly and that they had no hard feelings. All three later departed for parts unknown – still on good terms with the local law.

Good lawmen saw to it that the laws were enforced equally among both the high and low. On one occasion Ouray police officer Lem

Chelders was called to the exclusive Beaumont Hotel saloon to deal with a moneyed rowdy. The gentleman in question refused the officer's request to depart the premises, and, instead, threatened to whip Chelders. The lawman quietly laid his gun and badge on the bar, and after a hard fight, subdued the challenger and dragged him off to jail.

Although nearly everyone carried a gun during the 1870s, incidents with firearms were primarily due to lack of common sense or training and alcohol. Occasionally a drunk would open fire in a crowded saloon but was more likely to hit innocent bystanders than the target he was aiming at. For this reason shooting incidents were not tolerated, and potential troublemakers knew it. Consequently when there was a serious difference, it was most often settled with a knife, especially among immigrant mine workers who had little or no experience with firearms. By the early 1880s the carrying of guns was becoming the exception rather than the rule, and those who did usually opted for a small caliber weapon that could easily be concealed in a pocket.

Law officers themselves downplayed firearms. If they killed a suspect, most resigned and moved on, fearful of retribution from the dead man's friends. Few, if any, carried two pistols. The heavy, single-action weapons available at the time were far more effective when used one at a time, and few men needed more than a few shots to settle an issue. Most lawmen found it to their advantage to carry their gun as inconspicuously as possible, even concealed. Seventy-five percent of their arrests were related to drinking or fights over prostitutes. Where passion was involved, they did not want a situation to escalate any more than was necessary by an open display of firearms.

Alcohol proved to be a perpetual problem. If an out-of-control drinker could not be reasoned with, lawmen typically responded with a blackjack blow delivered to the side of the miscreant's head. Properly applied, it resulted in a knock-out. This device was typically a ten-inch leather tube that was larger on one end and filled with lead shot. The opposite end had a stout leather thong at the base of the handle that slipped around the officer's wrist. A second choice for a weapon was the standard police billy club, a fourteen-inch miniature baseball bat. Unlike the blackjack, the billy had more of a tendency to break bones. Once a man was subdued, the officer could apply a "chain twister" to the man's wrist and take him off to jail. This was a length of flexible chain attached at both ends to the bottom of a 'T' shaped handle. If a prisoner struggled, the officer would twist the 'T', and the chain would tighten around the offender's wrist. The pain would force a resister to his knees, and he would remain there with no further desire to struggle. Jail suddenly became a more desirable alternative.

Building a proper jail was expensive, so most towns typically had a small two-cell building constructed of wooden planks, usually rough lumber two inches by six inches, nailed one board on top of the other into the form of a box. A barred and locked street door opened into a narrow hallway. From the hallway each cell was entered through a separate door containing a small, heavily barred window. The cells had no openings leading directly to the street. Silverton operated for several years with a similar jail until a local grand jury determined that it should be closed because it provided neither heat in the winter nor ventilation in the summer. Sanitation facilities consisted of a bucket, although prisoners were allowed to have a variety of items needed to survive their incarceration including straight razors to shave with. Occasionally a despondent individual would slash his wrists or throat. Food was provided by a nearby restaurant or hotel. Eating houses often competed for feeding contracts, not just for the fifty cents per meal for breakfast and lunch and one and a half dollars for the evening meal, but because they could feed the prisoners left-over food that they might otherwise have had to dispose of without getting paid for it.

Much of a San Juan law officer's duty time was spent dealing with more humanitarian situations. They were on expected to be on hand when serious mine accidents occurred and were generally in charge of helping to locate and recover avalanche victims. Few ventured outside their own jurisdictions, unless they were escorting a prisoner to Canyon City or a mentally ill patient to the state institution in Pueblo. Because municipal budgets were usually tight, most lawmen were given wide latitude in dealing directly with offenders rather than relying on a court system. They preferred to settle an issue on the spot, even cases of petty thievery, hopefully to the satisfaction of all parties concerned. Property disputes were common. In one instance a newcomer to the Gunnison area bought a cabin that he was told was buried beneath the snow. Only the top of the stove pipe was visible. When the new owner dug down he found no cabin, only the length of stovepipe. He went to Sheriff Doc Shores and within a short time had his money back, and the issue was closed. Politics were another fence the area lawmen had to straddle. By the middle 1880s the temperance movement was strong in the San Juans. The "dries" wanted more control of the drinking houses. The "wets," led by the saloon owners, insisted on business as usual. The lawmen were often caught in the middle.

Occasionally a peace officer's conduct crossed the line. Animas City, located two miles north of Durango, was a small trailside town of some thirty houses, a few businesses, several saloons, and a school. Porter Stockton was hired as town marshal in 1880, and for several months the new lawman did an excellent job. Then he shot and wounded a man who refused to abide by the town's ordinance against carrying weapons into business establishments. Eyebrows were raised, but nothing was done. A few months later the marshal pistol-whipped the local barber for cutting him while he was being shaved. Angry residents unceremoniously ran Stockton out of town, and he headed for New Mexico. Unfortunately the region had not heard the last of the former lawman.

Being a San Juan police officer was not without its risks. A significant number of citizens were in the area precisely because they had had run-ins with the legal system elsewhere. A few had abandoned families. Mining camps were not the place to ask about a person's past, so upholders of the law had to depend, not only on personal skills, but on their inner intuitions as well. One of the most dangerous duties regional law officers faced was when they had to protect a prisoner from a mob. On occasion the mob won. Personal safety could be precarious for other reasons too. In 1881 a Lake City law officer was shot down and killed. A year later his replacement was wounded in a second gun battle. During the same time period, the Silverton town marshal was killed in a street shooting. Telluride had a former town marshal who was ambushed and murdered one night as he made his way down a dark street.

Criminal acts such as these were the exception. Most of the San Juan boomers had come to make money, not to willingly involve themselves in criminal activities. County records show court cases during this period averaging one per month, and these were usually civil rather than criminal. Such suits frequently involved problems resulting from poor surveying, overlapping mine claims, and water rights. To complicate these issues, individuals casually sold or bought property without filing and recording the necessary paperwork. Mine or claim owners were quick to bring trespass suits against anyone that they felt was infringing on their property rights. In one incident the Johnny Bull mine outside of Rico was claimed by two different sets of owners. One party would frantically work the mine until forcibly chased off by their rivals, who, in turn, would work feverishly to remove as much ore as they could before being chased off by the original group. This process was repeated several times to the satisfaction of no one. Finally the issue was settled peacefully in a court of law. The railroad town of Ridgway attracted a large Sunday crowd including area cowboys-young men who often drank too much. A typical Ridgway court docket for 1891 included the following: impersonating a police officer, disturbing the peace, speeding a horse-drawn carriage on the streets, obscene language, and discharging firearms within the town limits.

Judges were selected by popular election, and most had little legal training. If they wished to retain their position on the bench, it was to their advantage to render verdicts in accordance with local popular opinion. In the middle 1880s in Durango, a drunk staggered into the path of a buggy one dark night and was knocked down and injured. The driver, although not considered at fault, played the role of good Samaritan and took the man to a doctor who tended his injuries. The buggy driver even paid the fifty dollar medical bill. A short time later a local lawyer convinced the drunk, who had suffered no permanent damage, that he should sue the driver for two thousand dollars. Popular opinion was outraged, and both the lawyer and the drunk found themselves to be two of the most unpopular individuals in town. The judge refused to hear the case and threw it out. In another instance a judge in the Silverton area found a man guilty in a civil case a verdict expected by local citizens. The individual against whom the judgment had been delivered protested loudly that he would carry his case to the highest court in the land if necessary. The judge looked the man in the face and proclaimed that the case had already been heard in the highest court in the land. At nearly two miles above sea level, the magistrate had a point, but even more so, popular opinion had helped decide the case, and as far as most were concerned, that was as far as the issue would go. Serious crimes were dealt with in a similar manner.

Homicides netted prison terms of from ten to twenty years in Canyon City. A saloon keeper in the little track-side town of Sapinero shot and killed a patron, reason undetermined, and was sentenced to sixteen years in prison. A Creede prostitute, who had been habitually ridiculed by her boyfriend for her inability to play a good hand of poker, leveled a gun at her verbal tormenter and shot him dead. The jury reached a verdict of justifiable homicide and the woman went free.

The San Juans were not without a more notorious criminal element. Railroad construction sites were, perhaps, the worst. The men hired to lay the rails through the rugged mountains were prone to excessive drinking and the seeking of "amatory recreation" from track-side prostitutes. Alcohol and loose women made for a deadly combination and led to numerous shootings and stabbings. Con artists of every kind appeared when the track layers received their pay. Fortunately for permanent residents who lived nearby, track laying usually went quickly, and the criminal elements it attracted quickly moved on.

The mining camps and towns did have a few resident bad men. Generally these individuals and, in some cases, gangs, preferred not to attract attention to themselves. They dressed modestly, usually had a front of some kind, and many held honest jobs. Their criminal activities were more of a side line. Some proved quite successful. George Howard, an agent for Meserole & Blake's Stage Line, was a polished man with impeccable manners, yet for years he successfully and secretly masterminded a gang that operated in the region, stealing freight, high grade ore, and cattle. Eventually his activities caught up with him, and he was cornered near Grand Junction, Colorado. Attempting to escape shortly after his capture, Howard took a shotgun blast in the side followed by a rifle bullet in one shoulder. A deputy fired a final bullet into the outlaw's head, and the matter was closed.

Mine owners and freight companies were usually too clever to present opportunities to steal cash and bullion. In 1899 two masked bandits held up a stage between the Camp Bird Mine and Ouray, mistakenly believing that it contained a $12,000 bullion shipment. It did not, so in frustration they took the guard's saddle horse and were last seen headed for Utah. Occasionally a local lawman would supplement his modest salary by engaging in his own criminal activities. Jim Clark, a reputed former member of the Jesse James gang, worked as a deputy marshal for Telluride and did an excellent job. Unfortunately Clark also spent time outside of Telluride committing trail-side holdups. The scheme worked for a long time because the lawman was cautious to avoid anyone who might possibly know him and was always carefully disguised.

The San Juans did lay claim to a few professional gangs who operated openly because of the belief they were too mean to be messed with even by the law. A popular route into the San Juans lay along the rails of the Denver & Rio Grande Railroad from the San Luis Valley to Durango. It was common knowledge that many people came into the region carrying substantial amounts of cash, and that made them targets for the gangs. Train travelers had less to worry about, but numerous solitary travelers were robbed and some lost their lives. Occasionally they simply disappeared, never to be found again. The Stockton gang was the most notorious group to pursue such activities. It was headed by Ike Stockton who was a brother to Porter Stockton, the hot tempered former marshal of Animas City. After losing his marshal job, Porter dropped all pretense as to his real feelings for the law and rode with his brother. The gang began casually enough with trail-side robberies and cattle rustling "combination men" as they were called. If Colorado lawmen went after them, they slipped across the border into New Mexico and laid low until things quieted down. Northwestern New Mexico was sparsely inhabited at the time, mostly by former Texans busy carving out new cattle ranches. New Mexico had few lawmen to ride their side of the line. As the months passed the Stocktons grew bolder and the killings began. Things finally came to a head when three gang members entered Silverton on August 25, 1881. Confronted by the town marshal, one of the men drew down on the lawman and killed him. The killer and his friends fled, leaving behind a hapless individual who had ridden into town with them most likely unaware of who he had chosen as trail companions. Enraged townsmen, believing the newcomer to be one of the gang members, took the man into custody and lynched him. A $2,500 reward was offered for the actual killer, and Ike Stockton, the gang leader, turned his own man in and collected the reward. Silverton residents promptly lynched him too, determined to get things right. As it turned out, Ike had only a short time to enjoy his money before he was shot and killed in Durango for resisting arrest in another matter. The region had had enough of the Stocktons. In short order three more gang members were shot and killed, including the hot headed Porter. Two were captured and lynched in Colorado, and four more received the same fate across the state line in New Mexico. Porter Stockton's wife fired at a posse and was seriously wounded for her efforts. She never completely recovered and lived out the remainder of her life as an invalid. Another gang member was also shot, crippled, and received a long sentence in the Colorado State Prison. One more gang member went to prison, and a surviving comrade told friends that he had lived the outlaw life long enough, disappeared, and was never seen again. Citizens of Durango, caught up in the house cleaning, apprehended a few additional unsavory individuals and either shot or lynched them as well. By the middle part of 1882, criminal activity in the southern San Juans and along the New Mexico border had slowed down to a crawl. The Stocktons' brazen exhibition of lawlessness had lasted little more than a year and a half.

Cold blooded killings and brutal behavior on the part of most San Juan outlaws were more the exception than the rule. Most such individuals had been raised in God-fearing homes, and many times displayed their own sense of honor. They would willingly lift a watch from a robbery victim but would not take his gold wedding ring. They were more prone to pistol whip a victim than to shoot him. Most were lazy and had a tendency towards theatrics. A favorite form of recreation was to get liquored up and brag to an audience about their exploits real or imagined. Others proved so inept as outlaws that they nearly starved and ended up having to take honest jobs just to eat. A few became successful saloon keepers and bartenders. Nearly all had a deep respect for honorable women. A gang robbed a stage coach near Durango, and unaware of the proximity of local law officers, rode only a short distance before the entire outlaw band settled down to take a mid-day nap. Later in the Durango jail, the group was approached by Amanda Stollsteimer, the wife of a local rancher. She wanted to know why, although the gang had repeatedly stolen horses from area ranches, had they taken none of hers? Mrs. Stollsteimer was the proud owner of a number of prize breeding mares. Charlie Allison, the gang's leader, told the woman, quite simply, that he and his men did not steal from women.

Lawlessness continued in the San Juans, but it was more sporadic. In 1883 the First National Bank of Durango was involved in a bungled robbery attempt that left one bank employee dead. Occasionally bodies were found on lonely trails, beaten or shot to death. Such crimes were almost impossible to solve. In a few instances bandits would try to cover their acts by hanging a dead victim from a tree and pinning a note to the body warning other "thieves" that this was what might happen to them if they were caught stealing. This gruesome ploy was done in hopes the law would pass it off as an action by vigilantes, but lawmen were seldom fooled.

Vigilante committees did operate in the San Juans, although they preferred to be known as "Committees of Safety." Generally they acted through warnings and intimidations. A community troublemaker would find a neatly drawn card showing a tree with a noose attached and an open coffin sitting nearby. Beneath was the single word "forewarned." The drawing was considered necessary because many criminal types could not read. Most often such a warning accomplished what the committees hoped – the individual quickly left town. Silverton's vigilante group was more forceful: hooded and in the dark of night they would kidnap their intended target, escort him out of town, and make it clear that he was not to return.

Even the Ute Indians resorted to their own brand of justice on occasion. Forced to give up their traditional tribal holdings in Colorado a piece at a time, they frequently found trespassers on ground they still held legally by treaty. On one occasion during the winter of 1879-80, a group of Ute warriors surprised several cowboys grazing cows on the southern portion of the Uncompahgre Plateau, a clear violation of treaty rights. The well-armed Utes forced the cattlemen off their horses and onto their knees, where they were made to pick handfuls of the dry winter grass and stuff it into their mouths. The Utes grimly told the men that if it was good for the cows then it would be good for them as well. The warriors confiscated two quarts of whiskey from one cowboy's saddlebags and gave the trespassers time to ponder their eventual fate, while they shared the contents of the two bottles. Eventually they let the offenders go free with a warning.

Although vigilante groups did sometimes end the life of a miscreant, most hangings were the work of inflamed mobs rather than the committees themselves. The move towards mob violence was sometimes encouraged by local newspapers. The August 7, 1875, issue of the *Lake City Silver World* had this to say on the subject: "We are not particularly fond of violence, but we do not know anything that would afford our citizens more pleasure than the hanging of a horse thief." While a few horse thieves did end up with a noose around their necks, lynchings were generally reserved for perpetrators of particularly heinous crimes. In April of 1882 two saloon keepers from Lake City were surprised during a burglary attempt by the local, and very popular, sheriff. They shot and killed the officer but were taken into custody the next day. That night enraged citizens stormed the jail, took the two prisoners, and hanged them from a local bridge. The next day school was dismissed long enough for the entire student body to be marched down to see the two stiffened bodies still suspended from the bridge. One student wrote many years later that the incident banished any thoughts he might have had about pursuing a life of crime.

Two of the most widely publicized incidents involving mobs and criminals occurred in the town of Ouray. The body of a ten-year-old orphan girl was exhumed from a grave located on a ranch a few miles down the valley. Suspicions began when the girl had failed to show up at school a few days earlier and were intensified when the condition of the body indicated not only torture, but the strong possibility of sexual abuse. The girl's stepparents, Michael Cuddigan and his wife Maggie, were both arrested and jailed. As news of the situation spread through the community, horror was replaced by outrage. The jail was stormed, and the Cuddigans were taken and marched through the streets to the north edge of town. Mrs. Cuddigan was forced to walk barefoot through the snow, because it was believed that young Mary had spent her final hours without any shoes, locked in a freezing cellar with nothing more than a pile of straw to keep her warm. The couple were hanged at the north end of town, and the bodies unceremoniously buried in an empty field near the local cemetery. The lynchings sparked an outcry from the more civil minded elements of Denver, so the girl's body was exhumed and sent to the capital for a second postmortem. Denver authorities verified the original coroner's report, and Ouray's actions stood vindicated in the eyes of Colorado.

The second incident occurred a few years later following the opening of the lavish Beaumont Hotel in Ouray. A pastry chef, enamored of a pretty nineteen-year-old waitress who had rebuffed his advances, worked himself into a drunken rage and pumped four bullets into the helpless young woman. The perpetrator was immediately taken into custody and lodged in the town jail. Ellar Day was carried to her family home, and word of the shooting spread. Feelings began to intensify, and shortly after midnight an estimated one hundred armed and masked citizens demanded that they be given the keys to the cell where the prisoner was lodged. Deputy sheriff Myers refused. It was a brave act, but the mob persisted. When repeated sledge hammer blows failed to open the cell door, it was decided to burn the jail with the prisoner in it. In minutes the structure was in flames. More rational townsmen responded with fire fighting equipment but it was too late. The prisoner was dead. A short time later Ellar Day expired from her wounds, and a Durango newspaper, although deploring the way her killer had died, nevertheless lauded the fact that justice had been served – however crudely.

Such events, while gaining wide publicity, were the exception. Life in the silver towns was generally no more violent than would have been expected back East. In 1900 the *Telluride Journal* wrote that, up to that point, the town had experienced no lynchings, just one major bank robbery and only two or three murders in the preceding thirty years and this in a town with a boom-time population of over 7,000 people.

The San Juans witnessed one last surge of criminal activity in 1890 in and around the silver-rich town of Creede. The region went from zero population to over eight thousand in a matter of months. It grew so quickly that attempts to establish a working municipal government were overwhelmed. Parts of Creede were so untamed, during those first few months, that men passing dark alleys were murdered for the few dollars they carried in their pockets. Colorado newspapers proclaimed the town second only to Leadville for violence. Actual statistics recorded twenty murders in Creede from 1890 through 1893, mostly shootings and knifings, although one victim, staggering drunk was pushed into a creek where he passed out face down in the shallow water and drowned. Ironically what semblance of law and order Creede did have, at first came from the less than lawful themselves.

Jefferson Randolph""Soapy" Smith came to Creede from Denver, and he brought more than a dozen of his gang members with him. They dressed in black broadcloth suits, wore linen shirts, and displayed the best of manners. But in order to operate they needed a reasonably safe environment, both for themselves and their potential customers and

Dogs were popular in the San Juans.
Author's Collection.

victims. Their primary goal was to separate the unwary from their money as peacefully as possible, and that could not be done in an atmosphere of anarchy. Smith set himself up in his own gambling house and saw to it that his henchmen pursued their activities in a discreet manner so as not to arouse the ire of the more law-abiding elements of Creede. He made it clear to competing con men that they should conduct themselves similarly. Smith prowled the town on occasion, looking for crooked gambling games, whose perpetrators were threatened with death if they did not clean up their act. He provided help for unfortunate miners, looked after the financial needs of orphans and widows, and even helped sponsor the first church in Creede. Some called him the King of Creede. Then, within a matter of months, civilization caught up with the new town, and Smith began to lose his hold. He closed his gambling house and returned to Denver with his impeccably dressed gang still in tow. Later along with thousands more, Smith joined the Alaska gold rush in 1898. He settled in Skagway with his gang of toughs and was on his way towards controlling the town before being cut down in a late night gun battle with a rival gang. Smith, dead at age thirty-eight, left an estate worth less than three hundred dollars. Creede proved to be the last of the San Juan boom towns, and with the exit of men like William Randolph Smith, an era had passed.

CHAPTER TEN –
Sickbeds and Cemeteries

In the years that followed the Civil War, the American West was the scene of one new mining discovery after another. The mines needed railroads, the railroads needed farmers and ranchers, and rough and raucous towns were needed to provide services and supplies for them all. Accidents, injuries, and diseases were everyday occurrences. The West needed doctors.

The physicians who came during the early years were a diverse breed. Many were veteran doctors of the Civil War whose knowledge was often little more than the mechanics of amputating arms and legs and setting broken bones. In the case of disease, they were too often limited to dosing their patients with alcohol and narcotics in the hopes that the body would heal itself. In new towns, only a few months old, it was difficult or impossible for the patient to know much about the level of competence of a physician. State licensing boards were still years in the future. Consequently many doctors worked in an atmosphere of suspicion and mistrust.

The better medical schools in the East required three years of course work including a detailed study of physiology. On the other hand eastern diploma mills turned out physicians in as little as ten months; students who had never touched a cadaver, learning little more than symptoms and potential treatments. The average patient could not tell one diploma from the other. Congress briefly debated this issue and decided that the Constitution gave government no authority to intervene, so during the 1870s, frontier medicine was a situation of consumer beware.

By 1880 the West was settling down, and many of the medical incompetents had been weeded out. Young doctors, fresh out of medical school, came west with the ability to practice medicine on a level equal to that of their eastern counterparts. Despite their training, many mining camp physicians still found the western experience difficult. It took time to build clientele, sometimes months or years. Sometimes it never came at all. Many people preferred to do their own doctoring and would call a trained physician only when they knew they had exhausted all their own medical options. Many times it was too late, and the patient died despite a doctor's best efforts. This did little to further the reputation of formal medicine. Under these conditions it was difficult for mining camp doctors to make a living. To compensate, some opened drug stores and sold medicines, often combining their medical practices in the same building. Others hired out to mining companies and the railroads, where they dealt primarily with injuries and broken bones. Many became directly involved in mining. They went prospecting, even worked their own claims – but they were on call if their medical services were needed. Still others operated hotels, and a few tended bar. Since there were no trained veterinarians, people with expensive horses frequently called in local doctors to treat their ailing stock. A few came to be known as "horse doctors'" and the term was not meant, or taken, in a complimentary way.

When a doctor was called in for an illness, he had an established routine. The pulse rate was checked, and if it was elevated, the patient was generally and correctly assumed to be carrying a fever. Thermometers were available, but few western doctors owned or carried one. The skin and tongue were examined, and questions asked about the patient's appetite, and bowel and urinary action. The latter two functions were considered important, and doctors were quick to use cathartics to purge the bowel, and perhaps a diuretic consisting of a mercury compound to stimulate urination. The belief was that the removal of body wastes helped remove poisons that caused illnesses. Pathogenic organisms were still concepts of the future. Also popular were diaphoretics to force perspiration, and emetics to induce vomiting, again to remove toxins from the body. These approaches often worked, because many ailments of that day were brought on by eating tainted food or drinking bad water. Frequently, particularly for children, severe cases of intestinal worms were the problem. Doctors successfully combated this condition with a compound extracted from the aptly named wormwood plant. Trained physicians did have a variety of effective drugs and medicines that were used in treating certain diseases and ailments. Digitalis, a drug still in use, was favored for heart problems. Tincture of iodine was used to treat minor cuts and certain skin conditions. Carbolic acid had become the accepted agent to disinfect open wounds, although older doctors still relied on ordinary whiskey to accomplish the same task. A physician's medical bag contained drugs and chemicals that ranged from useful to worthless and safe to potentially harmful. Narcotics were carried in the form of opium, morphine and cocaine, as well as several bottles of "bitters," mixtures of alcohol or whiskey combined with various medicinal herbs. In addition there were sedatives and tonics.

Persistent illnesses of unidentifiable origins were called "wasting fevers," and doctors, in desperation, often used everything in their bag, hoping something might work. To break a fever the patient would be bundled in blankets to increase body temperature. Poultices were applied, and herbal teas administered. Along with his own efforts, a doctor frequently asked the family to pray for the benevolent intervention of higher and more knowledgeable powers than his own. Most physicians recognized their own limits.

One area where competent medical men felt at home was tending to broken bones. This was an injury that occurred frequently in both the mining and transportation occupations. Miners fell down shafts, and packers frequently had legs broken from the kick of an obstinate mule. Unfortunately X-ray machines were not invented until 1895, so bone setting had to be done by guess and by feel. Abdominal surgery, although quite risky, had become fairly common by 1875, especially for "knotted bowel" (appendicitis) if the doctor was called in before the organ burst.

Most physicians carried a leather satchel that contained the tools of their trade. In addition to powders, liquids, and pills, there were a lance, cutting knife, forceps, syringe, splints, ligatures, sponges (to mop up blood or body fluids and then rinsed out and used again on the next patient), bandages, plasters, caustics, a heating iron, sutures, a tourniquet, a catheter and a stomach pump. The catheter was primarily for men with venereal disease that had progressed to the point of shutting off urine flow. Prostitutes frequently overdosed on alcohol and narcotics or attempted suicide by drinking carbolic acid. The stomach pump was the preferred method for dealing with these situations.

Doctors also had to deal with gunshot wounds, a surprising number of which were accidental; others were often the result of a drunken moment of bravado in a saloon, dance hall, or bordello. Bullets in the extremities were seldom fatal unless a bone was shattered. In that case there was no way to reset the bone so that it would heal and contamination from bone and bullet fragments often led to gangrene. The standard solution was to amputate the limb immediately. Abdominal wounds were more serious. Pimps, prostitutes, and gamblers usually carried small concealed weapons seldom exceeding more than .32 caliber. Victims who survived for more than fifteen minutes were considered candidates for surgery. If they were drunk, the physician took advantage of that condition and performed the operation with no other pain killer. The patient was either tied or held down if conscious. If the patient was sober and conscious, a rag was stuffed into a drinking glass, chloroform poured onto the rag, and the glass inverted and held over the patient's nose until he or she passed out. At that point the surgery could begin. Abdominal surgery was seldom a sure thing even with a small caliber weapon or knife wound. A patient might survive, only to linger for days or weeks before expiring from infection. If a man had taken a bullet from a big .44 or .45 Colt or Remington, most doctors refused to even operate and made the patient as comfortable as possible, knowing that death would come in less than an hour from internal bleeding, no matter what they did.

Doctors filled other roles as well. Particularly during the early years of the San Juan mining boom, dentists were rare and even impossible to find in most of the region. So it fell to the doctors to deal with toothaches. Two treatments were available. A painful cavity might be dealt with by injecting it with pure carbolic acid and then stuffing it with a soft dental filling. This procedure worked only as long as the temporary filling remained in place. The more common method was to wrap a turnbuckle clamp around the decayed tooth and, while someone held the patient's head steady, the doctor would forcefully yank the tooth out. Hopefully the root would not break off in the process. If it did, the patient had no choice but to suffer months of agony as the remains were reabsorbed back into the body. Occasionally a subsequent infection resulted in death. By the middle 1880s itinerant dentists were traveling from town to town in the San Juans, dealing with the immediate dental problems in each community, and then moving on to the next. While their training was not that much superior to local physicians, most had begun to use nitrous oxide for extractions and were also beginning to provide permanent fillings for decayed teeth. Cavities were a problem because of poor diet and almost non-existent dental hygiene. Most individuals went through life without ever brushing their teeth. In some instances, people with dental problems took the train to Denver or Pueblo in search of dental care.

Train travel itself was touted as being healthy for a variety of ailments. The constant rattling, rocking, and jolting was said to provide 'passive exercise,' and this was considered especially healthful for women. To derive the most benefit, female passengers were advised not to wear excessively tight clothing, told they should not eat before sleeping, and sleep with their heads pointed in the direction of movement. Train travel was not without its hazards. Swirling cinders frequently found their way into the cars and into passengers' eyes. In severe cases, a drop of cocaine was placed on the eyeball to deaden it after which someone with a steady hand would use the tip of a wooden splinter or a knife point to remove the offending object.

Doctors also dispensed many of the medicines of the day. Drugs came in bulk and had to be broken down into the proper doses, not always an exact science. If materials came in powder form, which most did, a physician would determine proper dosage, separate the quantity with the point of his knife, and place it onto a small square of newspaper which would then be folded up and given to the patient along with necessary verbal instructions. Some practitioners went a step further and weighed out the ingredients and then formulated them into pills which were more convenient to handle and dispense. One physician by the name of Rowen, who practiced in Ouray during the early 1890s, went a step further and coded his pills with dye. Each type of pill was a specific color and meant for a specific condition. Prescriptions were usually a set price, regardless of what they contained, and could be quite expensive. Depending on how rich a mining district might be, prices often approached ten dollars per prescription – more than three days' wages for the average family. In addition there were fees for office calls and travel time. Generally most San Juan doctors followed prices set some years earlier in the mining towns west of Denver. A visit from the doctor cost from two to three dollars from the hours of 6:00 a.m. until 10:00 p.m. From the latter hour until six the next morning the price was generally five dollars. An office call during business hours was one dollar. When cash was scarce, many San Juan doctors would accept an equal value in firewood or other items.

The expense of dealing with a broken arm or leg averaged twenty dollars. Administration of chloroform cost five dollars, and a simple dressing for a wound averaged an even buck. The amputation of a frozen finger or toe set the sufferer back five dollars per digit, while the amputation of an arm or leg ranged from fifty to one hundred dollars, depending on where the cut was made.

Few people in the San Juans had any kind of medical insurance, and many could not afford large doctor bills, so all too frequently, attempts were made to deal with medical emergencies at home, on the trail, or even in the mine. It was not uncommon for workers and miners to have enough medical skill to set a broken bone or even perform an amputation. These were skills held primarily by Civil War veterans. But a time always came when a local doctor was called in, and they did the best they could with what they had at the time. Emergency surgery was performed beneath trees, in mine shafts and tunnels, on the tables of saloons, and on the grimy floors of stamp mills. Unfortunately many of the people they attempted to save died anyway of shock. Sometimes they had access to clean boiled water, sometimes not. They worked with inexperienced bystanders or family members who held lamps, administered chloroform, or kept flies away from the wound site.

By the early 1890s nearly all of the San Juan physicians were college trained. Sanitation had greatly improved, and most doctors, for that reason, had shaved off their traditional beards and mustaches. By 1899 most carried a copy of the *Merck Manual*, a 192-page book that gave instant access to symptoms and treatments for a wide variety of ailments ranging from asthma to excessive sexual cravings. For the most part they had gained the respect and trust of the people they served. Nevertheless doctoring in the pioneering days of the San Juans often proved a hard way to make a living for even the most dedicated of medical men and women.

Doctors found themselves in competition with traditions and patent medicines. Many people continued to rely on old frontier methods of dealing with their medical problems, "granny remedies" as some called them. Rendered fat from geese, bears, or skunks was used to rub into arthritic joints. Corn meal or grease was placed on burns; crushed sheep sorrel leaves mixed with gunpowder were applied to skin cancers. Lard was smeared on ringworm. Boiled pumpkin seed tea was taken to help expel stomach worms. Rusty nails were soaked in vinegar for several days before the liquid was given to women suffering from blood loss in childbirth. In this case, although crude, the concoction was as effective as anything else available for treating anemia. Wads of chewed tobacco were applied to a wound site to help stop bleeding. Tuberculosis was treated with iodine and turpentine rubbed into the chest. A pinch of snuff was forced up a woman's nose in the attempt to speed up difficult labor during childbirth. It was widely believed that three tablespoons of pepper stirred into a small glass of whiskey would sober a man almost instantly, and a sure cure for baldness was to drink a mixture of boiled whiskey, molasses, and tar several times a day. The age-old belief that many illnesses were caused or perpetuated by poisonous gases in the air, led to the practice of burning sulfur or tobacco in a sickroom. In cases of contagious diseases, care givers often placed a vinegar-soaked cloth over their noses before entering a sickroom. These practices continued to be used by many up to the turn of the twentieth century.

There were other remedies with a firmer footing in scientific fact. Various poultices made of red pepper or mustard gave relief for certain chest ailments. Sulfur and molasses were taken as a tonic. Laudanum (a tincture of opium) gave relief from pain and inflammation. Ipecac (made from the roots of a South American plant) was effectively used as an emetic. Quinine effectively treated chronic malaria or "ague" as it was known then. A variety of combinations containing carbonate of iron helped women suffering from anemia.

Oral patent medicines had become very popular by the early 1870s, and these were consumed in prodigious quantities by the self-doctoring crowd. Even trained physicians carried, advertised, and sold these concoctions. The most popular was "bitters," which used high strength grain alcohol steeped with a far ranging pharmacy of plants and herbs. It was not unusual for individuals, including church-going teetotalers, to become addicted to one of these products. By the latter part of the nineteenth century approximately 250 different derivatives of this nature were being marketed in the United States. They went by such names as Dr. Acher's English Elixir and Dr. Fahnestock's Celebrated Vemiguge And Liquid Opeldoc. Indian names were popular. There was Hooker's Wigwam Tonic, Kickapoo Indian Sagwa and Ton-Ko-Ko Tonic. Cough syrups ran a close second behind bitters. Pine Pinon Cough Cure was widely advertised, as was Indian Cough Cure and Kickapoo Indian Cough Cure.

An entire pharmacy of patent medicines were made just for women. There was Autumn Leaf Extract for Females, Dr. Brown's Renovating Pills, Sir James Clarke's Celebrated Female Pills and Dr. Simms, Arsenic

Complexion Wafers. The latter, popular among younger women, contained small amounts of arsenic and were recommended to be taken on a regular basis to ensure a blemish-free complexion. For the lady who could not quite put her finger on what ailed her, she could purchase a bottle of Pink Pills For Pale People or a bottle of Dr. Pierce's Favorite Prescription. Extremely popular was Syrup Of Figs, an excellent laxative, which was regularly advertised in San Juan newspapers.

Miners who had come to the conclusion that they were drinking too much might try Chamber's Remedy for Intemperance (it contained mostly alcohol) and a bottle of Aphroditine for suspected venereal diseases. Denver physician R. F. Price advertised in San Juan newspapers that he had a cure for all diseases arising from indiscretions of early youth. In most instances the partakers had no idea what was actually contained in the medicines they were consuming. Alcohol was usually the leading ingredient combined with opium or cocaine and various herbs. During the latter part of the nineteenth century it is estimated that one out of every 200 individuals in the United States suffered from an opiate addiction – many of that number being proper, middle class women. Raised in an era when a sense of Victorian prudery made it difficult or even impossible for some women to submit themselves to an examination by a physician, many preferred to place their trust in self-doctoring, advice from friends, and patent medicines. In the case of the latter, some formulas came with potentially harmful side affects. Dr. Rose's Obesity Cure was guaranteed to not only help a woman lose weight but to also speed up circulation. The active ingredient was atropine which, if taken in too great a quantity, could lead to a dangerously rapid pulse. Most patent medicines did not recommend limits. In fact many suggested that the patients take them as often as they felt the need.

Mail order catalogs took home medical care one step further by offering complete home medical kits that contained as many as sixty-five vials and bottles of everything from mercury to opium, phosphorus, nitric acid, and a selection of powerful laxatives. The latter were recommended to be given to children on a routine basis just as a preventative. As it became evident that a great deal of money could be made by competing with the established medical field, patent medicine increasingly became the domain of get-rich-quick quacks and frauds. In 1880 the *Solid Muldoon* in Ouray ran an ad for a patent medicine being marketed by one "Texas Tom" that was supposed to kill tape worms. The ad concluded that if the reader was not sure whether he or she had a tape worm to take the medicine anyway. The San Juans were one of the first places in the United States to see the industrial application of electricity, and this too found its way into medicine. Electric Liniment was a special secret formula through which an electric current had been passed. It was sold to treat rheumatism, cuts, sprains, sores of all kinds, and frosted feet and fingers. It and many other 'electric' medicines or devices proved popular.

Mining camp mothers tended to carry their reliance on patent medicines over to their children. Cold, drafty houses heated by stoves that often leaked harmful gases were one cause of illness. Continuous diets of heavy, fried foods was another. With no refrigeration, meat spoiled quickly but was often cooked anyway to avoid waste. Everyone in the family drank from the same tin cup or dipper, and bathing, particularly in the winter, was not a regular occurrence for anyone. Flies were a perpetual problem during the warmer months. Streets were littered with animal manure; pigs, chickens and other livestock lived in the back yards, and nearly every home and business had a pungent smelling outhouse not far from the back door. Window screens were not introduced into the San Juans until the 1890s, and it was almost impossible to protect food from flies, either in the pantry or on the table. As a result small children and babies, in particular, suffered from chronic gastrointestinal upsets. This condition, as well as typhoid fever, lessened near the end of the century when mothers began using pasteurized, condensed, canned milk rather than raw cow's milk that was contaminated with fly feces. But until then laxatives were the first line of defense against such disorders. Colic was treated with essence of peppermint in water. A sore throat could be dealt with by making a gargle out of one teaspoon cayenne pepper, two teaspoons salt, and two tablespoons vinegar, all mixed with one half pint of boiling water. Camphor pills were widely given as a preventative for colds, cramps, colic, diarrhea, and similar childhood ailments. Children were regularly dosed with patent tonics and worm syrups. Fevers were treated by wrapping the victim in cold, wet sheets. This practice often lead to further complications involving pneumonia. Then there were general cure-alls. Castroline was a special formula for infants that was guaranteed to cure fever, vomiting, diarrhea, teething problems, fretfulness, and intestinal worms. Supposedly it contained neither morphine nor opium. A nagging concern had existed for some time about giving opiates to small children, but the practice was widespread. For babies suffering from diarrhea there was Grove's Baby Bowel Formula, and for teething problems there was Mrs. Winslow's Soothing Syrup. The former concoction contained opium (which did slow down bowel action), and Mrs. Winslow's syrup harbored dangerously high levels of morphine, which certainly quieted a cranky baby cutting teeth, but side affects included constipation, vomiting, and a reduced breathing rate. Fatal overdose was possible. By 1900 it had become evident to national leaders that dangerous drugs and pharmaceuticals were being sold to the public. Many profit seeking drug manufacturers had also turned to adulterating their products to the point of ineffectiveness. In 1906 Congress passed the first federal law regulating the adulteration of drugs. It was not until 1912 that further legislation made it illegal to give false statements regarding the curative or therapeutic value of medicinal agents.

Pioneer life in the San Juans was often especially difficult for children. Cold winters, high altitude, and crowded, boom town conditions helped lead to higher than normal deaths among the very young. As many as eighty

Up to eighty percent of San Juan burials prior to 1900 were children under the age of five. Author's Collection.

percent of the burials in some of the mountain cemeteries before 1900 were those of children under the age of five. Some of the major killers included scarlet fever, measles, whooping cough, diphtheria, and dysentery. Cholera and small pox also made occasional but deadly forays into the San Juan towns. Diphtheria appeared most frequently and was said to be the greatest scourge in the West. This highly contagious respiratory ailment regularly affected more than 200,000 American children each year prior to 1925 with a death rate that exceeded 20,000. The disease sometimes claimed every child in a family, all within a matter of days. It was often brought to school by a student in the incubation stage, where he and every other child shared the same water dipper. By the time the original carrier became ill, the entire school had been exposed, and an epidemic was under way.

Desperate parents tried a variety of treatments as their children slowly began to choke to death from the mucus that built up in their throats. Sulfur was boiled in lime water and then dripped into the patient's nose. Others held the child upside down and inserted a feather soaked in goose grease

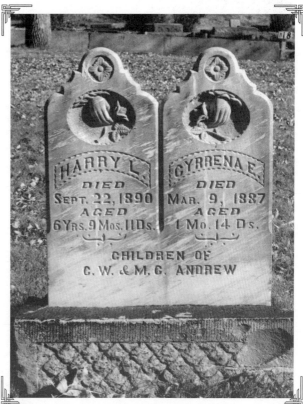

Children from the same family often shared a tombstone. Author's Collection.

deep into the throat until the victim vomited, hoping that would help clear the airways. Physicians favored the first treatment, although, in some desperate cases, they cut into the windpipe and physically removed mucus so that the child could breath again. This method brought relief, but infection from the incision often killed the patient in the end.

Grave markers for children were often elaborate and expensive. Author's Collection.

Cholera, usually carried by infected water, was another dreaded scourge. Symptoms began with stomach cramps (a frightening symptom mothers saw frequently in more benign ailments) and then quickly moved to the expelling of rice-water stools from the bowels followed by bloody diarrhea. Dehydration set in, and as the body was drained of electrolytes and potassium, muscle cramps became so severe that victims would scream in agony. Circulation slowed, eyes sank into the head, the skin began to grow cold, and death (which claimed fifty percent of cholera victims) usually came within twelve hours.

Smallpox was easily identifiable by the swollen, pustular eruptions on the body, face, and around the eyes. Patients would drift in and out of delirium, and small children, in particular, could not resist scratching at the sores. Desperate parents would tie children's hands to the sides of the bed to prevent them from scratching at their eyes and face. Lard was smeared on the sores in an attempt to prevent scars. A second treatment was to place carbolic acid on each lesion (which destroyed tissue and increased scarring), and then each raw sore was daubed with alcohol. The death rate from smallpox was also high. Parents fought these and other diseases with combinations of patent medicines and narcotics, sometimes administering larger and larger doses. An undetermined number of sufferers were overdosed and died from that condition rather than the disease.

Miners, freighters, and packers, while not adverse to seeking professional medical help, were apt to treat themselves and each other for particular conditions. Scurvy, brought on by the lack of vitamin C, was a frequent problem during the winter and spring months, but many former soldiers knew exactly what to do. During the pioneering decade of the 1870s, many San Juaners existed almost year around on diets of salt meat, soda biscuits, syrup, lard, and black coffee. Although they easily could have grown a limited amount of garden produce, few took the time. Mining was far more important. A Silverton resident recorded that his entire vegetable diet for the first three weeks of July, 1875, consisted of one onion. Teeth would loosen, gums would bleed, and wounds or injuries were slow to heal. If scurvy struck in the winter, the sufferer could turn to potatoes, because during the isolated San Juan winters fresh fruits and other vegetables were seldom available. Wild onions that grew on the mountainsides were also collected and used to treat the disease.

In the case of burns or scalds, the injured area was smeared with either linseed oil or axle grease. Olive oil was used for cuts and other raw wounds where the skin had been torn away. Sore muscles and mule kicks were treated with horse liniment. Whiskey was considered good for the common cold and rheumatism. Many times an undiagnosed ailment was called "mountain fever," and the sufferer would drink sage leaf tea mixed with whiskey. Because of heavy lifting, many miners and packers suffered from hernias. They made their own leather trusses, or had a doctor make one for them. In later years these devices were ordered from a catalog. If a hernia condition became too severe, the sufferer had to find another line of work. Most miners preferred to treat frost bite injuries themselves because they considered doctors too prone to amputate, especially fingers and toes.

Tuberculosis, or consumption as it was known then, was another common disease among working males in the San Juans, and the condition was made worse by working in damp mines, high altitude, and living in crowded bunk houses. Most workers chewed tobacco. Sand boxes were provided, but many chewers preferred to spit directly on the floor or out on the wooden sidewalks. Women's dresses, dragging through even dry spittle, would pick up the disease agent and carry it into their homes. As time passed a companion disease reared its head in the San Juans. Many of the mines were located in areas consisting of silica rock. As ore was mined, microscopically small dust particles, similar to shards of broken glass, filled the air. Inhaled into the lungs of a miner, they permanently lodged into the tissue causing severe scarring, loss of lung function, and eventual suffocation, usually before the age of forty.

Mines were extremely dangerous places to work for other reasons. Accidents occurred involving blasting powder and dynamite. Often when a charge would fail to go off, a miner would enter the chamber to check to

Unions and lodges often provided a miner's tombstone. Author's Collection.

see what had happened only to have the explosives go off in his face. Men sometimes violated basic rules and tamped a charge home with an iron bar rather than one made of wood or copper. A spark would set off a blast. Hoist and tram cables sometimes broke, boilers blew up, cave-ins occurred, and men fell down shafts. The standard way to bring an injured man off the mountain was to use the Civil War procedure of slinging two long pine poles with a blanket between two mules in the form of a litter. In many mining accidents, even a doctor could do little beyond administer morphine to make death come easier.

Heart disease was common among miners. High altitude with its subsequent decrease of oxygen, intense cold, and hard physical work helped exacerbate this condition. Statistics from Hinsdale County and the Lake City area show nearly one in ten deaths were attributed to heart disease during the years from 1875 until 1899. Often physicians would label such deaths as acute indigestion, the symptoms being similar.

Another disease found its way into the San Juans by the early 1890s. Influenza (then called grippe) came with an aching head, muscle pain, and fever. The word was French, meaning "to seize" because of the disease's rapid onset. Healthy individuals would usually recover in a few days, but infants and the elderly often contracted a form of pneumonia during the course of the illness and died. But it was pneumonia, or what was often perceived as pneumonia, that struck fear into the hearts of San Juaners both young and old. Nearly one in ten deaths in the San Juans were attributed to this ailment. Nearly any person who developed a high fever, rapid respiration, and a cough was believed to have pneumonia. Viral forms of the disease were present and generally fatal, but many times, conditions that expressed themselves in the lungs were actually other ailments. Silicosis and tuberculosis both weakened the lungs to the point that any additional strain could prove fatal. In other cases a miner would break a leg and develop a blood clot at the fracture site which then would travel to his lungs where pneumonia-like symptoms would be exhibited, and the man would die. Alcoholics whose vomit had entered their lungs developed a fatal form of the disease. Men who worked in the stamp and reduction mills were especially susceptible from breathing the fumes of the metals they were extracting, particularly lead which was present in nearly all of the silver ores. Gangrene, which was common, also allowed bacteria from the injury site to migrate to the lungs, and again the result was death. Whatever the initial cause, if symptoms appeared similar to pneumonia, then that was the diagnosis. Deaths from pneumonia or pneumonia – like symptoms occurred in the San Juans year around.

With nearly three-fourths of the work force single and living in dormitory style housing, it proved a serious problem to deal with the ill and the injured. In the Lake City area from eight to ten accidents or illnesses occurred each day that were serious enough to require a doctor's care. In response to conditions like these, the Order of Sisters of Mercy opened a hospital in Ouray in 1887. A similar hospital, by the same Catholic order, was opened in Durango, and others followed in the bigger San Juan towns. Mine owners deducted one dollar per month from each worker's pay in return for unlimited medical care, if and when needed. This took the sick and injured out of the company dormitories and into a more home-like atmosphere, where skilled nursing care was available.

Operating capital was always in short supply for the sisters who received nothing more than room, board, and a small allowance for personal necessities. If patients could not pay in cash, then produce and firewood were accepted, and charity was extended to those who had nothing. Each year members of the nursing order would visit the area mines to sign up new subscribers, but still, they were always short of cash to buy medical supplies and necessary equipment. The Ouray hospital was finally reduced to borrowing money from a Denver bank. When the sisters were unable to meet the conditions of the note, Tom Walsh, area philanthropist and the richest mine owner in the San Juans, paid it off. There were other risks for the sisters. In an 1884 smallpox epidemic in Durango, every sister in the hospital contracted the dreaded disease. The hospital closed for five months, and then reopened as the surviving sisters, pockmarked and scarred, returned to their duties. Records surviving from the Ouray hospital indicate that the facility admitted 998 patients during the first six years of operation. There were ninety deaths during that time, a respectable record considering that many of the patients were in extremely serious condition when they were admitted. Often, even when death was considered imminent, miners without families were taken to the hospital, because there was no other place for them to go. It was during those times that the sisters and the local priest ministered not only to dying bodies but to the souls of their patients as well.

Humorously it was said that the only piece of ground in the San Juans that was safe from claim jumpers and mining company lawyers was the six foot by two foot dimensions of a grave. The earliest burials were done without benefit of coffins. None were available. Instead small logs were cut and placed in the bottom of the grave to form a box open on the top and bottom. The bottom was then lined with grass or pine boughs, and the corpse laid in place. The top of the log box was covered with more logs, pine boughs, and finally dirt and rock. Markers were seldom more than a board or a pile of stones. In one case the grave of an avalanche victim was marked with one of his broken snowshoes. Most of these earlier burial sites have been lost but still lie along the major roads and highways that lead into the area today. As more people came to the San Juans, cemeteries and more formal burials became the standard. Coffins varied somewhat depending on the town. In Ouray they were usually rough pine lined with a fine weave cotton cloth. A pillow was provided, stuffed with pine shavings. Telluride coffins were nearly the same, but black calico was tacked around the outside. In Silverton the outside of the coffin was stained cherry red, although in an influenza epidemic in 1898 the town ran out of coffins and used rough pine boxes. When these were gone corpses were wrapped in blankets.

Bodies were kept no longer than three days, and in the case of saloon shootings or catastrophes, where the corpse was mangled or badly burned, the burial was often the same day as the death. Particularly for children, a damp rag soaked in soda was placed over the face to prevent discoloration. The deceased were washed and dressed in their finest clothing, and services were usually held in the appropriate church. In cases of community notables or multiple deaths, where large crowds were expected, other public buildings were used. The Wright Opera House in Ouray was the site for numerous funerals in that town. It was customary, particularly for various lodge members and popular citizens, that their cortege be preceded to the cemetery by one of the local bands. The newspaper could be counted on to provide a proper write-up for the deceased. In cases where burials were conducted in more isolated areas, people made do with what they had, but a clergyman was considered essential. In a burial near the top of Dallas Divide (west of Ridgway) a Methodist minister was called in to perform services for a Catholic woman. Catholic priests officiated at Protestant burials as well.

A Hispanic settlement that existed a few miles north of Durango had slightly different burial customs. The corpse was first dressed in night clothes, a cloth placed over the face, and the body then placed on a horizontal ladder in the home where a wake would be held the first night after death. The next day the body was carried to the burial ground. A grave was dug shorter than full body length with a small cave-like area at the end where the head would repose to protect it from direct contact with earth and rock when the grave was filled. A layman read prayers. Later when a priest was available, a second service was held. This community only lasted a few years, and today the location of the cemetery that contains approximately thirty graves, has been lost.

Not every burial was conducted with an eye towards propriety. When Joe Simmons, a companion of the infamous "Soapy" Smith, passed on in 1892 at Creede, he requested a joyous departure and no preaching. His friends obliged. In a blinding blizzard the casket slid off the back of the ice-covered wagon carrying it up to the cemetery. Followers scattered out of the way as it rolled and bounced down the hill. When it had been determined that the coffin's structural integrity had not been compromised, it was reloaded onto the wagon, tied securely, and the journey resumed. After the burial the gatherers sang Simmons' favorite ballads, shared several bottles of Pomeroy Champagne, and a few imbibers danced next to the newly filled grave. Creede had two cemeteries, one for Simmons and his crowd, and a second for more refined folks.

It was common to segregate burials. Pimps, prostitutes, and others of similar social order were often placed together. Miners were buried with miners. The wealthy and influential frequently shared the highest ground. Children were put to rest with other children. Many times the parents moved to other parts of the country when work ran out in the San Juans. At great economic hardship they often left exquisite tombstones to guard the graves of the little ones they had to leave behind. Carved angels and lambs appear frequently, as do lines of poetry and Bible verses. Often two or more children share the same monument, their deaths sometimes just days apart – the words diphtheria and pneumonia appear frequently.

Cemetery segregation continued for Protestant, Catholic and Jewish dead. Elks, Masons, Eastern Stars, Rebekahs and Independent Order of Odd

*Grave marker for Cora Holmes A Ouray prostitute who took her own life at twenty-five.
Author's Collection.*

Fellows all had sections within a cemetery for their members. It was only after the turn of the century that family burial plots begin to appear. Sometimes decades later, a widow of a miner would have her remains returned to the San Juans to rest beside her husband and often a child or two that she had left behind. European immigrants often had their remains returned for burial in the towns where they had first worked, often beside relatives who had preceded them.

San Juan cemeteries are often large, and many are still being used. Silverton counts more than 3,000 burials. The dead from surrounding mining camps and smaller towns were often brought in and buried. The *Red Mountain Mining Journal* reported in the spring of 1888 that, "The town is five years old and as yet there is no graveyard. Two children have died of unnatural causes. We should be contented." The two children mentioned had been buried in the Ouray cemetery.

There were also delayed burials. Avalanche victims were sometimes not recovered until the following summer, when the snow melted. In one slide that happened near the Virginius Mine in 1883, two bodies were buried so deep that they were not recovered for almost two years. Often avalanche or accident victims from high or distant mines were kept through the winter and brought down in the spring for burial. Sometimes individuals simply disappeared and were never found again. The vast and rugged expanses of the San Juans could hide a body very easily. In one instance a prospector from Silverton vanished, but his dog eventually came back to town. A search party followed the animal up one mountain and down another, until the animal finally worked his way to the bottom of a cliff and to the side of his dead master.

Funerals could be expensive, and often a man did not leave enough assets to pay for his own burial costs. These were borne by his companions who expected the same to be done for them. In 1900 a first-rate Silverton funeral involved the vehicle to carry the body and another to transport survivors. This service cost $12.00. Printing fees were $1.50, renting a band was $35.00, the minister was paid $5.00, and cemetery fees cost the same. A coffin and the undertaker fees were $75.00, and if the corpse was embalmed that was an additional $5.00. In the case of children, burial robes were popular. The robe would be folded over the body prior to the closing of the coffin. That was an additional $5.00. In instances where a miner left a wife and children, a collection would be taken up to send the survivors back east to their relatives. In some cases widows and their children were sent all the way to Europe. Frequently in the case of a young, single miner, the body would be sent east to his family. In Ouray preparation of the corpse and purchase of the coffin averaged $100.00, and transportation fees by train were about $65.00. For poorer individuals it was not unusual for a friend to make the coffin, open and close the grave, and keep other expenses minimal as well. Ministers and priests conducted services for members of their own congregations or parishes and the indigent at no charge. Head boards were made by hand; weathered, homemade tombstones still stand today, particularly in the old cemetery outside of Lake City.

Not everyone chose to spend their final rest in one of the San Juan cemeteries. Some preferred to have their cremated remains brought back to the mountains where they had spent their youth, and scattered on a favorite mountainside. Otto Mears's ashes were returned from California and scattered near Ouray. A granite monument to Mears was erected south of Ouray near the old Bear Creek toll station.

Today a visitor can wander through these old mountain cemeteries and learn a great deal about the early miners and their families just by reading the inscriptions, many of which are quite detailed. Very few of the San Juan pioneers died of old age.

CHAPTER ELEVEN –
Parsons and Priests

The glitter of gold and silver too often overshadowed spiritual matters among those who crowded into the mining camps of the early West. In 1879 a coastal California family packed up its belongings and set out for the nearby mountain mining town of Bowdie – known for its violence and drunkenness. Friends told the travelers goodbye and watched as the loaded wagon rolled down the dusty road. Still within earshot, they saw a little girl look back towards her former home and cry out, "Good-bye God! We're going to Bowdie."

Americans had become accustomed to the idea that mining towns were seldom more than temporary supply centers. They sprouted like mushrooms after a rain and faded away when the ore ran out. Often they were located in dry, windy, cold, and inhospitable places far from the influences of civilization. Nearly every inhabitant was there for one purpose – to make money in one way or another. Social amenities were scarce or non-existent. It was easy for the young miners to drink, gamble, and engage in pleasures not generally approved by more settled communities back East.

These conditions did not go unnoticed by eastern church and mission boards. Various groups responded by sending a token number of missionaries west, but that was usually the extent of organized involvement. Few denominations were willing to invest the time and money to construct churches, knowing that what might be built today would likely be abandoned tomorrow. The same thinking held true when silver was discovered in the San Juans. In the eyes of most, the new strikes in southwestern Colorado would also come and go, but the San Juaners saw it differently. Local visionaries believed the mines would produce silver for at least a hundred years. Almost from the beginning they began to build their towns with an eye towards permanence. Because of the technical challenges of the region, it attracted substantially higher numbers of educated managers, engineers, and technicians, many of whom brought their families with them. Their presence, in turn, attracted a higher caliber of businessmen and women who would not have been found in places like Bowdie. As in most mining towns, saloons, gambling houses, and bordellos were strongly in evidence, but so were various social and fraternal organizations. With children there was the need for schools, and at the insistence of wives and mothers, there was the call for churches. But eastern mission boards were still wary of investing much beyond nominal sponsorship for a handful of clergymen. If the San Juan miners wanted churches, the region would have to carry the load itself.

One of the first ministers to enter southwestern Colorado was Reverend George Darley. Darley came to Lake City in 1875, organized a Presbyterian congregation, spearheaded the raising of funds, and designed and built with his own hands the first church west of the Colorado Continental Divide. Some months later he walked to Silverton but found only one Presbyterian in the entire town, so he temporarily gave up hopes of establishing a church there. Instead he turned north to Ouray, preached a sermon in the White House Saloon, and collected more than two hundred dollars towards the construction of a Presbyterian church in that town. The congregation prospered and within a short time, had outgrown their building. They built

Pioneer preacher Rev. George Darley (on the right). Courtesy Ouray County Historical Society.

a larger one and sold their original home to the Catholics. About that same time a Catholic church was established in Lake City. Attendance at the Lake City Presbyterian church had grown to an average of 150 per Sunday, including members of other denominations who had not yet organized their own congregations. Lake City Baptists eventually built their own building, which they shared with the Methodists. Silverton, meanwhile, had developed active congregations of Episcopalians, Baptists, and Catholics. Reverend Darley was able to return and helped build a Presbyterian church as well.

A minister from Silverton hiked over Ophir Pass and down to Telluride to preach in Jim Hurley's Saloon each Sunday. Residents of the town, perhaps stung by barbs published in one of the Ouray newspapers about the saloon services, soon built Congregational and Catholic churches. To the south, Rico raised an Episcopal church during the first months of the town's existence. Other San Juan communities built churches as well, sometimes with unique features. Members of the Congregational church in Guston, between Ouray and Silverton, were called to worship both by a bell and a steam whistle. School buildings also doubled as churches in the smaller San Juan camps and towns.

Until the early 1880s San Juan clergymen were in short supply. Ridgway and Ouray were typical examples. With one priest between the two towns, Catholic services were held on alternating Sunday mornings in one location and that evening in the other. It was common for miners to walk or ride up to ten miles to attend services. Red Mountain Catholics had to get up early to walk to 9:00 a.m. mass in Ouray, nine miles away. Protestant worshipers were glad to have a clergyman in the pulpit regardless of his denomination. The Red Mountain town of Guston (with a population of 300) shared a minister with its neighbor, Ironton, located two miles down the road and with a population of 100. The Ironton church even had an organ. Communities felt that it was important to have at least one house of worship.

From the very beginning, the San Juan churches shared an ecumenical relationship with each other and the general population as well. Father J.J. Gibbons described the San Juaners as a mixture of "Mexicans, Scotchmen, Irish, Italians, Scandinavians, Austrians, sons of Cornwall and self-possessed Americans." Yet, he noted, while they might not always agree on day-to-day matters, they did exhibit respect for each other's religious practices.

Towns gave church groups building lots and even money. Newspapers ran ads encouraging readers to attend local religious services. Many of the bigger mines closed on Sunday to allow their workers free time to worship. Saloon pianists were frequently called on to play for Sunday church services. In Creede, noted by Denver newspapers as being the most violent of the San Juan towns, saloon patrons donated eight thousand dollars to build the town's first brick church. The fund drive was spearheaded by Creede's chief con-man and gambling king, "Soapy" Smith, who used his own money to pay for the organ. Smith occasionally attended services at the new church and suggested to his companions that they would be better people by following his example. It was a challenge that few accepted. They felt that they had done their share and were willing to allow others to listen to the preaching.

The churches themselves remained very much a part of the general community. They took turns sponsoring social events open to all who wished to participate. Such activities were well attended because they provided a touch of home, regardless of faith. The Durango Catholic Church sponsored a week-long fair each year. Members sold baked goods and handmade items, raffled off quilts stitched by the ladies, and concluded the event with a community dance. In 1895 the fair netted $752.13, which was applied to the parish's operating expenses that year – a figure which came to $1,696.90.

The mines all closed on Christmas Eve and everyone who could spent the night in one of the bigger towns. Different groups, particularly the Cornish miners, sang Christmas carols and hymns, as they wound their way down the steep mountain trails – as many as a hundred men at a time. High cliffs surrounding Ouray and Telluride provided a natural amphitheater effect, and those listening below said the impromptu choirs had an almost angelic quality. The Protestant churches held Christmas services early in the evening. Santa Claus appeared afterwards to hand out bags of treats. Each child received hard candy, nuts, an orange, and one small toy. The Silverton Catholic Church held a Christmas Eve midnight mass each year, which was open to all. The 1888 service was filled "to the door" with both Catholics and Protestants. Immediately afterwards the parish priest and one companion set out for Ouray. They followed the recently shoveled railroad track north over Red Mountain. It was snowing, and a wind was blowing as they hugged the cliff-side trail that wound down into Ouray, where they conducted a late Christmas morning service for a similar crowd of denominationally mixed worshipers.

If one church was in trouble, the others pitched in to help. When a disastrous 1889 fire in Durango destroyed four entire business blocks, it also reduced the Episcopal, Methodist, and Presbyterian churches to ashes. The surviving Baptist church opened its doors to the three congregations, and until they could rebuild, all four groups met in the Baptist sanctuary on a rotating schedule. During the late 1870s, when the temperance movement found its way into the San Juan towns, both the Protestant and Catholic churches joined forces in trying to rein in excessive drinking and the problems that came with it.

Winter was when church attendance increased dramatically. Most of the higher mines closed because of deep snow, and unemployed miners flocked into the bigger towns. Church services provided not only a spiritual uplift, but a welcome diversion that provided a chance to spend time with some of the local families. The little town of Sherman, nine miles southwest of Lake City, held inter-denominational prayer meetings on Saturday nights during the colder months and sponsored frequent Sunday musical concerts centered on hymn singing. Both activities were well attended.

San Juaners were quick to credit the Almighty for a variety of blessings. An eighty-year old cobbler in Ironton, a devout Catholic, liked to tell visitors and customers that he came to southwestern Colorado with no more than the clothing on his back. God had blessed him with continued good health, a prospering business, and two cabins he rented out. He, in turn, felt it was his duty to help others. The Golden Rule was practiced by even some of the San Juans' less ethical citizens. Bob Ford was a young Missouri gang member who had come to Creede in an attempt to escape the notoriety of having gunned down an unsuspecting Jesse James. A drunk and a bully, he was feared and had few friends, but he took on the expenses and care of an abandoned prostitute who was dying from tuberculosis. When the woman's end came, her benefactor also paid for the burial. A short time afterwards, Ford was gunned down. Reverend William Davis, who conducted Ford's funeral, later commented that the former outlaw's final send off was well attended, not from the notoriety he had received from shooting Jesse James but because of the unselfish compassion he had shown for a dying woman.

Those who ministered to the spiritual needs of the San Juans were themselves compassionate men who often risked their lives to be at the bedside of someone who was sick or approaching death. It was not unusual for a clergyman to ride, walk, or ski up to ninety miles to conduct a mission of mercy, and often in the foulest of weather. They frequently teamed up with mail carriers, each lending the other support in traversing through some of the deadliest avalanche country in the world. Until the early 1880s it was not unusual for a man of the cloth to spend an average of three days a week in the saddle. Their biggest complaint was their knees. Hours of relative immobility in the saddle, cold temperatures, and summer rains took their toll. Arthritic joints were constant companions for some. On the trail these men of God dressed no differently than those they served, some carried firearms, and on occasion, they proved good with their fists. But in their saddlebags were the vestments and paraphernalia of their trade.

Easter cards were more popular than Christmas cards in the late 1800s. Author's Collection.

Catholic priests carried holy oils, a chalice, bread, and wine. The constant, grueling pace turned them into savvy and excellent mountain horsemen, who rode short legged, stocky animals with stamina and the ability to negotiate treacherous trails in all kinds of weather.

Indeed it was weather that often proved the greatest enemy. When Father J.J. Gibbons rode down into Ouray from Silverton through a raging blizzard, he was asked how the trip had been. His tongue-in-cheek reply, "in the usual way without any more serious inconveniences than being obliged to shovel snow, open the road and help drag out the horses from the high drifts." The Silverton to Ouray road could prove incredibly treacherous during winter. In 1884 another Catholic priest left Silverton and headed for Ouray to give last rites to a dying woman. The seventeen mile journey took him four days. On the way back to Silverton he was caught in an avalanche and swept down the mountain, but, bruised and battered, he managed to dig his way out and continue on. Ironically telephone service linked many of the San Juan towns and camps together very early, and it was by this means that the hard-traveling priests and preachers were often summoned. Whether they went sometimes became a judgment call. If death appeared imminent through injury or pneumonia, the clergymen usually set out no matter what the weather conditions; even then the deep snows and howling winds sometimes defeated even the most determined of men and forced them to turn back. They were also called out during mine disasters and found themselves riding or hiking up unfamiliar, ice-covered mountain trails in the dark of night. Many times they were on hand to help search for avalanche victims. Their presence gave comfort to the search parties, who hoped that the Almighty would not let the mountain run again and carry away a priest or minister. These rescuers were often the same men who during the Civil War had thrown away their playing cards prior to going into a major battle in an effort to bargain with God to spare their lives. In emergencies such as avalanches and mining accidents, it was common for Episcopalians and others to be given last rites by a Catholic priest and at no protest from the deceased individual's companions.

Many among the clergy felt it their duty to visit the mines during the warmer months on a regular basis. They were fed and put up for the night at no expense to themselves and usually conducted services of one kind or another that evening. Often someone produced a violin, and those gathered would join in the singing of hymns, ballads, and even popular songs of the day. Catholic priests held catechism classes for the children in the smaller camps and towns when they were passing through.

Priests received a small stipend from the Catholic church, and Protestant ministers and missionaries often existed on irregular funds provided by the people they served. What they received was often too little to meet the high expenses of living in the San Juans. As a result a wide network of homes, cabins, and mines existed across the region, where a clergyman could find food and shelter at no expense to himself. Miners made it a point of honor to see that clergymen were paid for conducting funerals and weddings of their friends. Stables loaned horses or put up a clergyman's own animal for free — or gave at least a fifty percent discount. Railroads gave clerics a free pass on their lines, good for anyplace, anytime, that the company had track. San Juaners generally took a very protective view of all men of the cloth. Still it sometimes proved difficult to survive, particularly for the Protestant clergy. Many worked secular jobs on the side, and a surprisingly large number were carpenters, often designing and erecting the very buildings they preached in. Others, like Mormon missionaries F. C. Warnky and his wife, supported themselves in Lake City in the early 1880s by operating a photography studio.

It was difficulties such as these, as well as the extreme hostility of climate and terrain, that discouraged all but the most dedicated men of the faith from even coming to the San Juans. Those who did were usually set apart from their eastern counterparts by a greater sense of compassion and dedication. They willingly preached in saloons and reached out to any and all in need. Pioneer preacher Reverend George Darley regularly ministered to his charges in establishments where many of the righteous of that day would never have gone, but such boldness had its rewards. His first convert in Lake City was an orphaned, twenty-year-old prostitute. Darley and others of his calling were frequently asked to perform funeral services for women in the flesh trade. Few San Juan churches would allow a prostitute's coffin inside their building, so the clergy went to the bordellos instead. Burial sermons were routinely used to goad the living into reexamining their own lives. When a Silverton woman, caught in an unhappy and abusive marriage, passed on, the officiating priest faced the mourners and said, "In a moment of folly she contracted an alliance with one who, in station and culture, was her inferior, and reaped the fruits of her imprudence in an unhappy married life."

Despite the fact that most people in the San Juans had known each other only a few months or years, the area had a strongly developed sense of community that was often strengthened by the clergy or by religious beliefs in times of tragedy. In 1878, at a mine above Silverton, an accidental explosion left one man dead, one blind, two severely injured and crippled, and another in such a state of emotional trauma that he died two years later in the hospital for the insane in Pueblo. These five Moyle brothers had not only been popular residents of the town but had also regularly played as a one-family band at local dances. The incident left the close-knit community in shock, but they tended to the survivors and saw to it that the widow and five orphans of the man killed had money enough to return to England. It was times like these that the towns and camps turned to their clergymen for leadership and support. That support continued in other ways as well.

It was common for many miners, young and single, to spend no more than a few years in the region before returning east or moving on. Ministers and priests alike felt their duty was not so much conversion and church building but rather to establish a defense against excessive drinking, crime, and prostitution. Most of the San Juan miners had been brought up in families where religion was important and moral standards strict. The mining camps with easy access to alcohol, gambling, and loose women proved to be tempting experiences far from disapproving eyes back East. Both priests and ministers felt that they were obliged to convince the mining town crowds that while their loved ones might not be watching, God was.

An occasional older gambler or saloon keeper sometimes disagreed with that idea, even to the point of fists, but most younger men showed a respectful deference to members of the clergy. Visiting eastern journalists came to the San Juan towns expecting to see an avalanche of hell and violence, but they reported that while drinkers and revelers were allowed to express considerable liberty from sundown on Saturday night until sunup the next morning, Sundays saw control of the towns and camps revert to the families and church crowds. Saloons, gambling houses, and bordellos were open, but they kept a low profile. During the week most potential customers, after a twelve hour work shift, were either too tired, too broke or too far away to allow for treks into town.

Clergymen also served as unpaid social workers. They frequently secured the release from jail of young miners and placed them in the homes of older parishioners who were willing to reacquaint them with the rules and canons with which they had grown up. Through the post office the clergy were also recipients of letters from parents, sweethearts, and wives back East inquiring as to the whereabouts of their loved ones. Often this would involve tracking the party down and serving as a go-between in attempts to bring family members back together again. In other instances it was the contrite offender who came to the clergyman to request that he write the first letter east or even to Europe to attempt a reconciliation.

Consumptives who came to the San Juans in hopes of curing their diseased lungs often ended up financially impoverished and unable to work. Frequently they threw themselves on the mercy of clergymen who shouldered the responsibilities of seeing that care was provided until death. There were also the needs of individuals critically injured in mine accidents. The building of hospitals went far to deal with this problem and most were operated by Catholic sisters who saw it as their duty to tend not only to the the bodily needs of their charges, but their spiritual conditions as well. If an unchurched individual came under their care, he often left, dead or alive, a Catholic. Father Gibbons recorded of the nursing sisters that, "I have often been struck by the wonderful conversions that occur at our hospitals. Men who spend long lives in utter spiritual abandonment are suddenly touched by the merciful hand of God, and the Divine visitation, which they regard as a curse, becomes the greatest blessing."

By the early 1890s it appeared that the eastern mission boards from two decades earlier had been proven wrong. The mines were still producing. Prognosticators continued to claim that the silver mines would last a century or more. Many of the earlier wooden churches had been replaced by larger ones of brick or stone. Congregations and parishes had grown exponentially as more families had moved into the region, replacing much of an earlier boom time generation that had since moved on. The San Juans were prospering and with them the churches, but for those not blinded by the glitter of silver pouring from the mines, insidious signs were beginning to appear. Years of ever-increasing production from the West's silver mines had left an unusable surplus of the white metal, and the nation was entering the initial stages of a serious financial depression. Within a matter of months the bell and steam whistle that called the faithful in for Sunday Services at Guston would be silent. An era was ending.

CHAPTER TWELVE –
An Era's End

The year 1890 was one of exuberance for the San Juan region and for all of Colorado. The federal census reported that Denver had grown, in just ten short years, from 35,000 to more than 106,000 people. Pueblo (Colorado's second largest city) had increased from 3,000 to 24,000. Empty prairies were filling up with farms and towns. Rutted trails and lumbering processions of ox-drawn wagons had been replaced by steel rails and iron engines. Colorado was on the move, and nowhere was that more evident than in its southwestern mountains. Two trains a day steamed into Lake City bringing consumer goods and mining machinery. Flour that had been carried in by mules a dozen years earlier at $25.00 to $30.00 per hundred pounds now cost $1.75. A dozen pressed glass goblets, that would have sold for $3.50 fifteen years earlier, were now retailing for 40¢. Drinkers, who had paid $10.00 a bottle for low quality whiskey at the beginning of the San Juan rush, could now imbibe brand-name products for as little as $2.50 a quart. As early as 1887 fresh lettuce was advertised in Durango grocery stores at Christmas. Store owners gave easy credit to almost anyone, buoyed by the incredible quantities of silver, gold, copper, lead, and zinc that continued to pour from the mines.

Unlike so many of the earlier boom and bust cycles across the West, the San Juan mines were proving rich beyond belief, and cash-flush owners poured large portions of their profits into advanced mining technology, hoping to increase their fortunes still further. On June 21, 1891, a switch was thrown at a new hydroelectric plant outside Telluride, and for the first time, alternating current was fed through wires more than two and a half miles up a mountain to the Sheridan Mine. Moments later a telephone call came back to the electric plant – the motors were running. The benefits of electricity soon extended into the towns. Businesses of all kinds had come to count their profits, not on current revenues, but on future expectations based on the perceived benefits of silver production. The Silverton Railroad saw its profits nearly double from 1889 to 1891, and similar increases were expected to continue. The line itself spared no expenses. Guests in the dining car could order Breenbrier Bourbon Whiskey, imported French and German wines, and Russian caviar at reasonable prices.

A miner's lunch pail at the Montrose County Museum. Author's Collection.

Culture had come to the San Juans. In February, 1888 the Red Mountain Lyceum and Dramatic Association gave its first performance with songs, guitar solos, and an oration from part of Shakespeare's King Richard III. The event was well attended. A year later Silverton organized the Silverton Jockey Club, an excuse, some said, to provide a flashier social life for the growing number of wealthy elite in the town. Social stratification, rare during the pioneer days of a decade earlier, was becoming more evident. Yet even here, the lines were never completely drawn. Each Christmas, "Captain Jack" Stoiber, (as she was known) the wife of a wealthy Silverton mine owner, would purchase presents for every child in town and deliver them in a sleigh pulled by two magnificent bay trotters. Mrs. Stoiber, herself from humble beginnings, was said to be able to handle her team of horses as well as any man and could outdo mule skinners when it came to creative uses of the English language.

For the legions of working men there was baseball for relaxation, and local teams had recently adopted the 1889 national rules of three strikes and four balls. Mine workers avidly followed activities in the National League, and game scores were telegraphed in from the eastern states within minutes of play and were carried in the local papers the next morning. Silverton's town band had gained a state-wide reputation and played frequently in Denver – always taking a burro with which they gave packing demonstrations to adoring crowds. In August of 1892 San Juan members of the Knights Templar joined forces for a train ride to Denver to participate with fellow lodge members in a state convention that included a parade, banquets, and a grand dress ball. Nor was the traffic to Denver just one way. Candidates for state and national office had begun including the San Juans in their campaign schedules. The mountain circuit proved no hardship on the politicians, because the San Juans were becoming known for some of the finest hotels in the West.

The Silverton Imperial Hotel (later called the Grand Imperial) opened in 1880. Mirrors came from Paris, and other furnishings were custom made

An early day medical device at the Ouray County Historical Museum. Author's Collection.

and imported. The saloon in the Imperial never closed, and its safe was never locked until one night by accident. An expert had to be brought in from Denver to open it, because no one had bothered to save the combination.

One of Durango's centerpieces was the Hotel Strater, which opened in 1882; it was so plush that wealthy local citizens rented rooms during the coldest weeks of winter, primarily to take advantage of its modern, central heating system – something few Durango homes had at the time. The fourth floor of the Strater (reserved for hotel help) was off limits to guests, but this merely provided a challenge for adventurous male guests who sought "midnight entertainment" in the rooms of amenable housemaids.

Gunnison had the La Veta Hotel, which opened in 1884. The four-story structure had 107 sleeping rooms and a grand staircase built in Europe of walnut, ash and oak. Floors were covered with carpets from Turkey. Unfortunately the hotel was so large and expensive to operate that it encountered almost immediate financial difficulties.

In July 1887 Ouray witnessed the grand opening of the Beaumont Hotel, not only furnished with the very latest in opulence but fully electrified and supplied with endless hot water piped in from nearby hot springs. On opening night employees and staff were sent in from the famed Palmer House of Chicago to see that everything went as planned. Some Palmer House staff members were so impressed, they quit their jobs in Chicago and stayed on at the Beaumont. The *Solid Muldoon* reported that the hotel was "the finest finished in the country." Rooms were available for eight dollars a night, and guests dined in an exquisite two-story dining room, while being entertained by an orchestra seated in a second story gallery.

Like the Beaumont, other San Juan hotels took advantage of the numerous hot springs located throughout the region and, in some cases, built entire resorts around them. In 1890 the Cebolla Hot Springs Resort north of Lake City opened with a hotel, private cabins, bath house, and soaking pools. It proved popular not only with locals but tourists as well. Area railroads, anxious to increase profits, had begun advertising nationally about their San Juan tours. The region was extolled for its incredible scenery – much of which could be seen comfortably from the windows of a train car. Wealthy easterners came in increasing numbers, as well as groups of vacationing college students and Europeans. Visiting journalists extolled the beauty of the high, rugged mountains. The region's reputation continued to grow and over the years such notables as Lily Langtry, Lillian Russell, King Leopold of Belgium, and President Theodore Roosevelt checked in at places like the Beaumont and the Silverton Grand. During the warmer months of 1889 over 10,000 visitors toured the San Juans. More hotels were built, less opulent than the Beaumont and the La Veta, but comfortable and charging four dollars or less per night. Some even began allowing local prostitutes to take meals in the dining rooms – provided they dress properly, remain sober, be polite, and avoid contact with other guests. For travelers who wished to explore the mountains, area ranchers provided buckboards, horses, and guides – all for a price. Although costs seemed reasonable for seasoned travelers, one local custom did raise their eyebrows. If an area merchant was handed a five dollar bill, he most likely would give change in silver dollars. Easterners preferred paper silver certificates. Some had never seen the actual metal coins and hesitated taking them, fearful they might be counterfeit. Indirectly they had reason to be suspicious.

In 1873 the United States, following the lead of many European nations, had abandoned the bi-metal standard of minting sixteen dollars in silver for every dollar in gold and had gone completely to a gold standard. The price of the yellow metal had been fixed at $20.67 per ounce, but the price of silver was allowed to fluctuate with market demand. The laws of 1873 did provide for the minting of silver dollars to be used in foreign trade or, by law, as legal tender for American debts of less than five dollars. Western mining interests reacted to these events with alarm, but for several years, commercial, and international demand continued to keep the price of silver high. In 1877 it sold for $1.20 an ounce. But warning signs began to appear as more nations abandoned the bi-metal standard for that of gold. Silver prices began to fluctuate. Western mining states petitioned Congress and won a partial victory when law makers passed the Bland-Allison Act of 1878, which legislated that the government would buy and coin from two to four million dollars per month in silver coins. The price of silver continued to reflect market values, and mint production rarely exceeded two million dollars in silver per month. In two years the metal had dropped to $1.05 per ounce. A few months later it lost another thirteen cents. Again the western silver interests began twisting arms in Congress. Their reward came in 1890 with the passage of the Sherman Silver Purchase Act in which the government agreed to buy four and a half million ounces of silver each month, still at market price, but the volume nearly equaled national monthly production at that time.

Mining interests in the San Juans watched these events with a mixture of optimism and trepidation. Telluride alone was shipping close to 150 train cars of silver concentrates every thirty days. In the spring of 1891 a glut of ore had piled up near the mines on Red Mountain awaiting rail transport. Extreme snows that winter had prevented the ore from being moved out on a regular basis. To complicate matters still further, a new and incredibly rich silver strike had been made in the eastern San Juans near the town of Creede. Within weeks a new railroad was hauling millions of dollars in additional silver ore to already overworked front-range smelters. To help handle the increased volume of raw ore, more concentrating mills were built

An ore car at the Ouray County Museum. Author's Collection.

near the mines. The Creede strike gave renewed impetus to prospectors, and San Juan newspapers cheered them on. When a strike was discovered at Carson, a camp located a few miles south of Lake City, the *Creede Candle* wrote, "Carson is a wonderful section. It is developing itself and says to the world I am the Eldorado...," What the paper failed to say was that Carson was too remote, extraction too costly, and extreme weather year around made the entire venture risky. Still the search for silver continued. Every time a rumor surfaced in towns like Ouray, a new round of mining property speculation could be expected. In some places every foot of ground had been claimed in hopes it might be sold to outside investors or other speculators and always at a premium. For the producing mines the objective was immediate profits, and as the price of silver began to deteriorate, production was increased. The warnings given by management that increased production also meant increased production costs and higher debt loads, were largely ignored.

The Populist Party (western in origin and committed to the unlimited coinage of silver) gained control of the Colorado Legislature and governorship in 1892 and sent both of Colorado's representatives to Washington to do battle with eastern industrial interests who were afraid that too much silver would devalue the national currency. Support was growing to repeal the Sherman Act. In an impassioned speech Horace Tabor, the silver king of Colorado, made a plea to national leaders, "You wipe silver off the face of the earth and you just double the value of gold and the gold securities and the debt securities, which will have to be paid in gold."

But interest in western mining problems was being upstaged by an ever increasing number of business and banking failures in the East during the spring of 1893. As the crisis continued to grow banks began calling in loans from over-extended businesses and this led to still more financial collapse. Silver itself was caught up in the avalanche. Production increases and upgraded technology had been increasingly financed with borrowed money. Mines began closing in Colorado, and they dragged a number of local banks down with them. Unemployed miners journeyed to the new and as yet unaffected gold fields of Cripple Creek hoping to find work. Others crowded the streets of Denver and were temporarily put up in tents and fed with public money. Afraid of possible riots, the railroads were pressured to provide reduced or free fares to transport the growing legions of the jobless to points further east.

Financial panic was becoming world wide and in June, India (an important silver importer) ceased production of silver coinage. In four days the price of silver dropped from $.83 to $.62. More Colorado mines closed. An

Aspen newspaper proclaimed that the situation was bad but could not get much worse. The statement proved premature. Eastern gold interests, with the support of President Cleveland, were increasingly placing the blame for financial difficulties on western silver. A call to repeal the Sherman Act was beaten back in June but throughout the summer the national financial crisis continued to grow. Finally on October 30, 1893, Congress repealed the Sherman Act. The news was telegraphed west, and within minutes the price of silver dropped to $.50 an ounce.

Out of 895 Colorado mines, 435 were now closed, and 45,000 workers connected with the state's mining industry were without jobs. Within weeks entire towns in the Colorado mountains were emptied out. To make matters worse, the state's farmers and ranchers were in the midst of a serious drought. Crops would not grow, and there was not enough feed for their livestock. Worse, many farms and ranches were heavily mortgaged. Banks began to call in these loans as well. The nation was in the beginning of what would become four hard years of economic depression. Few places were hit harder than the towns and mines of southwestern Colorado.

Wealthy San Juan silver barons had invested heavily in Denver real estate. Unable to keep up their payments, the banks began calling in the barons' notes. Men who had been rich one day found themselves paupers the next. Business establishments in the mining towns lost their cash flow when customers they had extended credit to, in ever increasing numbers, were either unable to pay or fled town, often in the dead hours of night. In a fight to survive, most businesses lowered prices almost to wholesale in an attempt to pay off their own creditors. Even this approach proved too little, too late for many. Restaurants and other service-related enterprises no longer had enough customers to keep their doors open. Even prostitutes saw their incomes disappear. A few of the older ones committed suicide.

The mines that closed ordered the families living in company housing to leave, often in a matter of days. On Red Mountain the population dropped from 3,000 to fewer than 700 in less than a year. A year after that the town of Red Mountain burned and was abandoned. Rico's population was decimated as nearly 5,000 of its 6,000 inhabitants moved away, and nearly all of its low grade mines closed, unable to even make expenses. Durango suffered as demand for its coal declined, and layoffs occurred at the local smelter.

But the decline in silver prices had not affected that of gold. The metal remained at more than twenty dollars an ounce and increasing amounts of gold-bearing ores were being discovered in the San Juans. One of the first big strikes had been made near Ouray in 1889 at the American Nettie Mine. Incredibly rich ore allowed the owners to install their own hydroelectric plant and power the mine entirely with electricity. The expenditure kept operating costs low, and, perhaps more important, kept money flowing into the town of Ouray. Three years into the silver crash, mining entrepreneur Thomas Walsh discovered an even richer deposit of gold nine miles southwest of Ouray. The new Camp Bird Mine produced gold ore valued at more than $3,000 a ton. Silver had given birth to the city of Ouray, but it was gold that saved it. Silverton also turned to gold, and although the town suffered, it survived. By 1897, one half of its output was gold. Telluride, a technological jewel of American mining, faltered, then found its economy steadied by gold. Even old mine dumps were reworked in an effort to reclaim enough yellow metal to keep men in jobs and companies in business. Although it proved a grim time for most, optimism did not completely die. In 1895 the New Sheridan Hotel was built in Telluride. The cherrywood bar came from Austria and many of the furnishings from Paris. There were two dining rooms; the most elaborate was separated into sixteen velvet draped compartments, each furnished with a telephone with which to summon the waiter. Although the town survived and mining activities continued, the glory days of silver were over.

Many of the mining consortia that did survive in the San Juans were interested in squeezing out every cent of profit possible. With a surplus of unemployed miners, there was little difficulty in finding men willing to work longer hours at lower pay, and often under more dangerous conditions. A steady decline in relations between management and labor began to assert itself. Men who would never have stolen ore from previous mine owners they liked and respected, began to have second thoughts about filching it from faceless eastern conglomerates and stockholders they had never met. Juries that a few years earlier would have almost never found men guilty of high grading, now sent them to the penitentiary in Canyon City for attempting to take a few pieces of ore home in their lunch buckets.

Thomas Walsh provided the exception. A long time Colorado resident who had pulled himself up from the status of a working miner to one of America's new rich; he saw to it that his Camp Bird miners were treated properly. Walsh not only paid his men well, but also ensured that they had the very best in living conditions at the mine. A three-story boarding house was steam-heated, lit with electric lights, and boasted hot and cold running water and the very latest in flush toilets and porcelain bath tubs. In the dining room his employees ate off china rather than from the customary tinware most mine boarding houses used. When an avalanche destroyed the elegant structure, Walsh promptly had it rebuilt in almost identical fashion. He was also generous to the city of Ouray, including building and equipping the town with one of the finest libraries in the state.

Silver supporters continued to cling to the hope that the metal would regain its previous position and watched as the election of 1896 drew nearer. Eastern industry continued to hold steadfast to the gold standard, while western mining and small business interests agitated for the return to silver. Their champion was a Nebraska orator named William Jennings Bryan, who earlier gained national fame in a speech that warned that if America continued to follow the path laid down by eastern industrialists and bankers, the nation would be crucified on a "cross of gold." Silver champions cheered, and Bryan was nominated to run as president on the Populist ticket. Even the Democratic party was split on the silver issue, and Silver Democrats threw their support behind Bryan. The Nebraska orator did not fail to include the struggling miners in his campaign circuit and spent time in the San Juans appearing before ecstatic crowds.

The drought that plagued parts of the nation continued as well. During the summer of 1896 hundreds gathered at Bayfield, near Durango, for a two week revival meeting which included prayers for rain. But for the moment rain did not come, nor did enough support for Bryan. Although he handily carried Colorado and other mining states by a margin of six to one, eastern interests won out, and Republican William McKinley, a gold supporter, carried the election. Silver's last hope was gone.

Gold continued to dominate Colorado's mining industry but at a price. Labor and working conditions continued to decline. During the height of the 1893 depression, Cripple Creek gold miners under the newly organized

Western Federation of Miners went on strike in hopes of obtaining better wages and working conditions. When the affair threatened to turn bloody the mine management caved in, and the miners won a partial victory. In 1896 another strike was called in Leadville about similar concerns, but it was beaten down by management, and the concessions that had been won at Cripple Creek were rescinded. Continuing unrest persuaded the Colorado Legislature to limit the working day to eight hours for all miners, mill, and smelter workers. Meanwhile in the San Juans economic conditions continued to worsen. In 1898 the famed Yankee Girl mine on Red Mountain, one of the richest silver producers in the world, shut down its pumps and allowed its shafts and tunnels to flood. A few weeks later the Silverton Railroad closed down. Then trouble began in the mines near Telluride.

Mine management had begun paying miners by a complicated formula based on how much ore they produced rather than a set daily wage. This cut further into their already declining standard of living. In 1901, 250 angry miners laid siege to the Smuggler-Union Mine. Guns blazed and contingents of state militia were called in to prevent further bloodshed. The violence ended with minor concessions being made to the workers, but Telluride continued to simmer and fearful investors began pulling their money out of the area. Finally on October 31, 1903, violence erupted when management began hiring non-union workers to staff the local mills. State leaders, fearful that these actions would spread beyond Telluride, called in the Colorado National Guard. Martial law was declared, and scores of union leaders were arrested and deported with orders never to return. Management again held the upper hand, but the Telluride troubles had done more than pit labor against management. Long time Telluride residents had taken sides, and friends had turned on friends. Bonds that had held firm for nearly a third of a century were broken.

Although mining in the San Juans would continue well into the new century, nothing would ever be the same. Even Ouray's population declined from 2,000 in 1893 to 1,200 by 1902. Other San Juan towns suffered similar declines. The fine Western Hotel of Ouray, built in 1891, closed in 1893, and then reopened in 1895. Its owners made ends meet by catering weddings and banquets. The mighty Beaumont had reduced its room rates from eight dollars a night to three, although instances of opulent living could still be found. One of Tom Walsh's managers lived in the hotel with his wife and dog. A local butcher sent fresh T-bone steaks to the manager's suite every day but Sunday – for the dog.

Nationally the San Juans were now a western backwater. The nation had emerged from the 1893 Depression with renewed vigor, but her interests were focused on foreign expansion and international commerce. Western gold and silver had been all but forgotten. Thousands made an effortless Atlantic crossing to visit the Paris Exposition in 1900, while many in the West still talked of taking six months to cross their own continent by covered wagon thirty years earlier. Now they could make the same journey by train in six days. Electric lights and motors, which had been pioneered in the San Juans, were now lighting and powering many of America's cities and factories. Automobiles were appearing in increasing numbers. Men had taken to the air in strange contraptions called aeroplanes. Doctors were able to peer inside the human body with X-ray machines, and people were viewing moving pictures and listening to music in their own homes on phonographs. Few stopped to realize that it had been western silver and gold that had financed the foundation for this new age of technology.

Meanwhile miners continued to tunnel and blast ore from beneath the granite peaks of the San Juans. They withstood a recession in 1907 and lived through another round of mine and business closings. This new period of hard times took the remaining wealth of David and Laura Swickhimer, who years earlier had gone from poverty to riches when they discovered one of Rico's richest silver mines. The Swickhimers had sold their mining interests for more than a million dollars before the silver crash and had invested heavily in the Rico State Bank. When it failed in 1907 they stoically watched as the last of their wealth was doled out to bank depositors. Ironically, San Juan silver production continued strong through 1920, but the price hovered around the $.53 mark. For most, mining provided only a bare living and oftentimes not even that. By 1920 Rico's population had dropped from the thousand survivors of the 1893 crash to less than 300 souls. One by one the remaining mines across the San Juans shut down. The Sunnyside, outside Silverton, was the last survivor, and it ceased production in 1991.

Over the years snow and fire reduced the giant concentrating mills to scrap iron and rubble. The iron was loaded up and carted away during World

War II scrap metal drives. Ghost towns were also stripped of iron. Even the fire hydrants were dug up and carried off to the steel mills. Fine brick mansions, long empty and in a state of decay, were torn down and salvaged for the brick. Many of the little camps and towns totally disappeared, not even leaving a trace by the turn of the twenty-first century.

Mining companies still retain control of thousands of acres of claims and hundreds of miles of underground tunnels in the event that the price of silver might someday reach a level to allow the richer mines to reopen, but as the years pass, that option appears less likely. To glimpse the economic future of the San Juans one needs to stop on a summer day in the Animas Canyon and listen to the rhythmical chuffing of a steam engine and the shrill scream of its whistle echoing off the cliffs above. Trains that once hauled ore and freight between Silverton and Durango now ply the same route loaded with tourists who, for a few hours, breath the acrid fumes of burning coal and view the same breathtaking scenery once shared by travelers from an earlier time. On nearby mountainsides, evidence of those days can still be seen – mostly mounds of rock and rubble. The nearby slopes, once cut clean of trees for shoring timbers and firewood, are again covered with maturing pine forests.

When winter comes the trains only run to Rockwood, safe from the avalanches that rumble down the steep cliffs south of Silverton. A different breed of tourist replaces those of summer. On cloudy nights lights twinkle from the windows of the remaining San Juan towns and the ski lodges at Telluride and Purgatory. The air comes alive with snowflakes that will be the champagne powder of the next morning, but beyond these tiny pockets of human activity, winter holds the mountains tightly in its grasp, and the San Juans sleep beneath a blanket of pristine whiteness.

BIBLIOGRAPHY

A

Abbott, Carl. *Colorado: A History Of The Centennial State.* Boulder, CO: Colorado Associated University Press. 1976.

Armstrong, Betsy R. *Century Of Struggle Against Snow.* Boulder CO: University Of Colorado. 1976.

Arps, Louisa Ward. (Ed.) *Faith on the Frontier.* Boulder, CO: Weekly Enterprises Inc. 1976.

B

Becker, Raymond M. *Guns Along the Silvery San Juans.* Cañon City, CO: Master Printers. 1975.

Backus, Harriet Fish. *Tomboy Bride.* Boulder, CO: Pruett Publishing Co. 1969.

Bancroft, Caroline. *Six Racy Madams of Colorado.* Boulder, CO: Johnson Publishing Co. 1965.

Benham, Jack. *Ouray.* Ouray, CO: Bear Creek Publishing Co. 1976.

Benham, Jack. *Silverton.* Ouray, CO: Bear Creek Publishing Co. 1981.

Benham, J. L. Camp Bird and the Revenue. Ouray, CO: Bear Creek Publishing Co. 1980.

Bennett. Edwin L. and Spring, Agnes W. *Boom Town Boy.* Chicago, IL: Sage Books. 1966.

Bird, Allan G. *Bordellos of Blair Street.* Pierson, Michigan: Advertising, Publications & Consultants. 1993.

Bird, Isabella L. *A Lady's Life in the Rocky Mountains.* Norman, OK: University Of Oklahoma Press. 1960.

Blair, Rob. (Ed.) *The Western San Juan Mountains.* Niwot, CO: University Press Of Colorado. 1996.

C

Carver, Jack, and Others. *Land Of Legend.* Denver, CO: Caravan Press. 1959.

Chapter, Sarah Platt Decker. *Pioneers of the San Juan Country.* Colorado Springs, CO: The Out West Printing and Stationery Co. 1942.

Collman, Russ. *The R.G.S. Story: Over Bridges...Ridgway to Telluride. Vol. I.* Denver, CO: Sundance Publications, Ltd. 1990.

Cross, Roselle Theodore. *My Mountains.* Boston, MA: The Stratford Co. 1921.

Crossen, Forest. *Western Yesterdays. Vol. II.* Boulder, CO: Boulder Publishing Co. 1964.

Crossen, Forest. *Western Yesterdays. Vol. III.* Boulder, CO: Boulder Publishing, Co. 1965.

Crossen   Forest.   *Western Yesterdays.*   *Vol.*   *IV.*   Boulder, CO: Boulder Publishing, Co. 1966.

Crossen, Forest.   *Western Yesterdays.*   *Vol.*   *V.*   Boulder, CO: Boulder Publishing Co. 1967.

Crum, Josie Moore. *Three Little Lines. Durango, CO: Durango Herald News.* 1960.

Crum, Josie Moore.   *The Rio Grande Southern Railroad.*   Durango, CO: Hamilton Press, Inc. 1961.

D

Dallas, Sandra.   *No More Than Five in a Bed.*   Norman, OK: University of Oklahoma Press. 1967.

Dallas, Sandra.   *Colorado Homes.*   Norman OK: University Of Oklahoma Press. 1986.

Darley, George M.   *Pioneering in the San Juan.*   Community Presbyterian Church of Lake City, Colorado (Private Printing). 1976.

Delta County Independent (1895 Brochure Reprinted 1973).   Delta, CO: Courtesy of the Delta County Historical Society.

Dorset, Phyllis F. *The New Eldorado.* New York, NY: The Macmillan Co. 1970.

Dunlap, Richard.   *Doctors Of The American Frontier.*   Garden City, NY: Doubleday and Co., Inc. 1965.

F

Fairfield, Ula King.   *Pioneer Lawyer.*   Denver, CO: The W. H. Kistler Stationary Co. 1946.

Fay, Albert H.   *A Glossary of the Mining and Mineral Industry.* Washington, D.C.: Washington Printing Office. 1920.

Fiester, Mark.   *Look For Me in Heaven: The Life of John Lewis Dyer.*   Boulder, CO: Pruett Publishing Company. 1980.

Fossett, Frank.   *Colorado.*   (Reprint from 1880) Glorieta, NM: The Rio Grande Press, Inc. 1976.

Fritz, Percy S.   *Colorado: The Centennial State.*   New York, NY: Prentice-Hall, Inc. 1941.

G

Gardiner, Charles Fox.   *Doctor at Timberline.*   Caldwell, ID: The Caxton Printers, Ltd. 1938.

Gearhard, Dona. (Ed.)   *Journal of the Western Slope.*   *Vol.*   *7, No.*   *1.*   'The Western Hotel of Ouray.' Grand Junction, CO: Mesa State Printing Services. Winter 1992.

Gibbons.   Rev.   J.J.   *In the San Juan.*   Chicago, IL: Calumet Book and Engraving Co. 1898.

Gray, Thorne. *Quest For Deep Gold.* La Grange, CA: Southern Mines Press. 1973.

Gregory, Doris H.   *History of the Wright Opera House.*   Long Beach, CA:

Cascade Publications. 1983.

Gregory, Doris H. *Ouray's Historical Hospital and Today's County Museum.* Long Beach, CA: Cascade Publications. 1987.

Gregory, Doris H. *The Town that Refused to Die: Ridgway, Colorado.* Ouray, CO: Cascade Publications. 1991.

Gregory, Doris L. *Ouray County Cemeteries.* Ouray, CO: Cedar Hill Cemetery District. 1996.

Gregory, Doris H. *Ouray's Beaumont Hotel.* Long Beach, CA: Cascade Publications. 1997.

Gregory, Marvin. and Smith, P. David. *Mountain Mysteries.* Ouray, CO: Wayfinder Press. 1987.

Gregory, Marvin. and Smith, P. David. *The Million Dollar Highway.* Ouray, CO: Western Reflections, Inc. 1997.

Griffiths, Thomas M. *San Juan Country.* Boulder CO: Pruett Publishing Company. 1984.

H

Houston, Grant E. *Cemeteries of Hinsdale County, Colorado 1874-1995.* Decorah, IA: The Anundsen Publishing Company. 1996.

J

Jocknick, Sidney. *Early Days on the Western Slope of Colorado.* Denver, CO: The Carson Harper Co. 1913.

K

Karoleuitz, Robert F. *Doctors of the Old West.* Seattle WA: Superior Publishing Co. 1967.

Kushner, Ervan F. *Otto Mears: His Life and Times.* Frederick, CO: The Platte Press. 1979.

L

Lavender, David. *The Telluride Story.* Ouray, CO: Wayfinder Press. 1987.

Lewis, Marvin. (Ed.) *The Mining Frontier.* Norman, OK: University of Oklahoma Press. 1967.

Look, Al. *Unforgettable Characters of Western Colorado.* Boulder, CO: Pruett Publishing Co. 1966.

Look, Al. *Bits of Colorado History.* Denver, CO: Golden Bell Press. 1977.

M

McKinstry, Hugh Exton. *Mining Geology.* New York, NY: Prentice-Hall, Inc. 1955.

McLean, Evalyn Walsh. *Father Struck it Rich.* Ouray, CO: Bear Creek Publishing Co. 1981.

Mangan, Terry William. *Colorado on Glass.* Denver, CO: Sundance Ltd. 1976.

Marshall, John. and Roberts, Jerry. *Living (and Dying) in Avalanche Country.* Silverton, CO: A Simpler Way Book Co. 1993.

Monroe, Arthur W. *San Juan Silver.* (Place of publication and printer unknown). 1940.

Mund, Mary D. *Women Physicians of Colorado.* Denver, CO: The Range Press. 1976.

Murray, Andrew E. *The Skyline Synod: Presbyterianism in Colorado and Utah.* Denver, CO: Golden Bell Press. 1971.

Myers, Sandra L. *Westering Women and the Frontier Experience 1800-1915.* Albuquerque, NM: University Of New Mexico Press. 1982.

N

Nossaman, Allen. *Many More Mountains. Vol. 1.* Denver, CO: Sundance Books. 1989.

Nossaman, Allen. *Many More Mountains. Vol. 2.* Denver, CO: Sundance Publications, Ltd. 1993.

O

O'Rourke, Paul M. *Frontier in Transition. Colorado State Office.* Denver, CO: Bureau Of Land Management. 1980.

P

Pederson, Freda Carley. *Over My Dead Body.* Norman, OK: Levite of Apache. 1996.

R

Rathmell, Ruth. *Of Record and Reminiscence.* Ouray, CO: The Ouray County Plaindealer and Herald. 1976.

Rickard, T. A. *Across the San Juan Mountains.* Ouray, CO: Bear Creek Publishing Co. 1980. (Originally published in 1907). Edited. *Ridgway Recipes and Remembrances.* Ridgway, CO: Ridgway Community Pride. 1990.

S

Sammons, Loline. *They Came to Powderhorn.* Gunnison, CO: Wendell's Print Shop. 1981.

Saxton, O. Glenn. *Colorado and its Mining Industry (1859-1959).* Denver. CO: Mining And Petroleum Committee. Colorado State Chamber Of Commerce. 1959.

Scarinzi, Dr. H. J. *(Interviews January and February 1999)* Hugo, Colorado. Seagraves, Anne. *Women of the Sierra.* Hayden, ID. Wesanne Publications. 1990.

Seagraves, Anne. *Soiled Doves – Prostitution in the Early West.* Hayden, ID: Wesanne Publications. 1994.

The Sears, Roebuck Catalogue 1902. (Reprint) New York, NY: Bounty Books. 1986.

Smith, Duane A. *The Birth of Colorado.* Norman OK: University Of Oklahoma Press. 1989.

Smith, Duane A. *Durango Diary.* Durango, CO: The Herald Press. 1996.

Smith, P. David. *Mountains of Silver.* Ouray, CO: Western Reflections, Inc. 2000.

Smith, P. David. *Images of the San Juans.* Ouray, CO: Western Reflections, Inc. 1997.

Stedman, T. L. *Stedman's Shorter Medical Dictionary.* (Place of publication not listed) Wilcox and Follett Co. 1942.

Stewart, George. *The Sowing and the Reaping.* Caldwell, ID: The Caxton Printers, Ltd. 1970.

Stollsteimer, Robert S. and Causey, Dorothy. *Christian and Amanda.* (Place of publication not listed) F.E.R.S. Books. 1996.

Stone, Donald B. and Others. *Introduction to Epidemiology.* Madison, WI: Brown and Benchmark Publishers. 1996.

W

Weber, Rose. *A Quick History of Telluride.* Colorado Springs, CO: Little London Press. 1974.

Wolle, Muriel Sibell. *Stampede to Timberline.* Chicago, IL: The Swallow Press, Inc. 1974.

Wolle, Muriel Sibell. *Timberline Tailings.* Chicago, IL: The Swallow Press, Inc. 1977.

Wommack, Linda. *From the Grave.* Caldwell, ID: Caxton Press. 1998.

Wood, Frances and Dorothy. *I Hauled these Mountains in Here.* Caldwell, ID: The Caxton Printers, Ltd. 1977.

Wright, Carolyn and Clarence. *Tiny Hinsdale of the Silvery San Juan.* (Place of publication not listed) Big Mountain Press. 1964.

Wyman, Louis. *Snowflakes and Quartz.* Silverton, CO: Simpler Way Book Co. 1993.

Y

Young, Otis E., Jr. *Western Mining.* Norman, OK: University of Oklahoma Press. 1970.

Young, Otis E., Jr. *Black Powder and Hand Steel.* Norman, OK: University of Oklahoma Press. 1975.

INDEX